Michael Overdiek
Meike Susten

100 business ideas for start-ups

bup

Michael Overdiek
Meike Susten

100 business ideas for start-ups
Volume 2 of the series:
Revolution of business start-ups without capital

ISBN: 978-3-68904-175-5 (paperback)
ISBN: 978-3-68904-185-4 (e-book)

Volume 1: Using artificial intelligence and innovative methods to develop new business ideas (978-3-68904-154-0)
Volume 2: 100 business ideas for start-ups
Volume 3: The realisation of business start-ups without capital (ISBN: 978-3-68904-194-6)

Copyright: Bremen University Press, Bremen
The manuscript may not be used in whole or in part without the prior written consent of the publisher.

First edition
April 2024
Version 1.0
Printed in the European Union
bup@bremenuniversitypress.com
www.bremenuniversitypress.com

Michael Overdiek
Meike Susten

100 business ideas for start-ups

Contents

INTRODUCTION TO VOLUME 2 — 5

THE BUSINESS IDEA — 8

STRATEGIES FOR IDENTIFYING NICHE MARKETS AND UNMET NEEDS. — 12
CONDUCT MARKET RESEARCH — 13
UTILISING CUSTOMER FEEDBACK AND SOCIAL MEDIA — 14
CARRY OUT A COMPETITIVE ANALYSIS — 15
DEVELOPING PROTOTYPES AND MVPS — 16
NETWORKING AND INDUSTRY EVENTS — 17
AGILE DEVELOPMENT AND CUSTOMISATION — 18

100 BUSINESS IDEAS EXPLAINED — 20

IT SERVICES — 20
IT SUPPORT AND CONSULTING — 21
ARTIFICIAL INTELLIGENCE AND MACHINE LEARNING — 26
SOCIAL MEDIA MANAGEMENT — 34
WEBINAR AND ONLINE COURSE PRODUCTION — 36
PODCAST PRODUCTION AND CONSULTING — 38
SEO CONSULTING — 39
DIGITAL ART AND DESIGN — 41
ONLINE COMMUNITY MANAGEMENT — 42
DIGITAL PRODUCTIVITY CONSULTING — 44
PERSONALISED GIFT DESIGN — 46
ONLINE MUSIC LESSONS — 48
REMOTE TECH SUPPORT — 51
DIGITAL ARCHIVE MANAGEMENT — 53
E-SPORTS TRAINING AND COACHING — 56
WEB DEVELOPMENT AND DESIGN — 58
IT SUPPORT AND MAINTENANCE — 60
PODCAST EDITING — 61
DEVELOPMENT OF MOBILE APPS — 63

CYBERSECURITY CONSULTING	64
CLOUD COMPUTING SERVICES	65
DATA ANALYSIS AND REPORTING	67
SOFTWARE DEVELOPMENT	68
BLOCKCHAIN DEVELOPMENT	70
DIGITAL MARKETING AND SEO	72
ARTIFICIAL INTELLIGENCE (AI) AND MACHINE LEARNING	73
FREELANCE DATA ANALYSIS	75
COUNSELLING AND COACHING	**77**
PERSONAL TRAINING AND COACHING	77
ONLINE EVENT PLANNING	79
CONSULTANCY FOR REMOTE WORK AND VIRTUAL TEAMS	80
SELF-DEFENCE COURSES	82
CONSULTANCY FOR SUSTAINABILITY	84
E-LEARNING PLATFORMS AND CONTENT	86
CRAFT AND PRODUCTION	**88**
SUSTAINABLE FASHION	88
ENVIRONMENTALLY FRIENDLY AND SUSTAINABLE BUSINESS MODELS	**90**
VIRTUAL TOUR GUIDES	90
TRAVEL PLANNING, ONLINE TRAVEL AGENCY	91
EVENT AND EXPERIENCE OFFERS	**93**
MOBILE CATERING AND FOOD TRUCKS	94
EVENT PLANNING AND COORDINATION	95
LEISURE ACTIVITIES AND WORKSHOPS	97
SUSTAINABILITY SERVICES AT FESTIVALS	98
SERVICES	**100**
HOUSE AND PET SITTING	100
MOBILE ANIMAL CARE	102
PLANT CARE AND ADVICE	103
IOT SOLUTIONS (INTERNET OF THINGS)	105
VIRTUAL INTERIOR DESIGN	106
VOICE SERVICES	108
ENVIRONMENTAL COUNSELLING	110
NUTRITIONAL COUNSELLING AND MEAL PREP PLANNING	111
FOOD DELIVERY SERVICE	113
PHOTOGRAPHY	115
LANGUAGE TEACHING	116

Babysitting and childcare	118
Garden maintenance and landscaping	120
Dropshipping	122
Rental of equipment	123
Domestic help and cleaning service	125
Private tuition	127
Translation services	129
Art hire and sale	130
Specialised cleaning services	132
Personal development and life counselling	134
Leisure activities and workshops	135
Virtual property assistance	137
Virtual event planning	139
Creative writing and ghostwriting	141
Content Creation	142
Health and wellness services	**144**
Personal training and fitness	144
Online fitness courses	145
Nutritional counselling (see above under services)	147
Educational programmes on various nutrition topics.	147
Yoga studios and meditation courses	148
Services to promote relaxation and mental well-being	150
Massage therapy	152
Mental health, psychological counselling and therapy	153
Education and training	**157**
Language and cultural coaching	157
Courses and workshops	159
Retail and e-commerce	**161**
Affiliate Marketing	161
Online marketplace for local products	162
Online sale of vintage and second-hand items	164
E-learning platforms and content	166
Craft	**168**
Handmade products	168
Upcycling and restoring furniture	170
Mobile car wash and valeting	171
Bicycle repair and maintenance	173

4

Introduction to Volume 2

The spirit of entrepreneurship without substantial capital illuminates an increasingly important perspective in today's business world. This concept emphasises that it is possible to start and run successful businesses with minimal financial resources. At the heart of this approach lies the ability to utilise innovative ideas, techniques and a willingness to break new ground. At a time when the financial hurdles to starting a business often seem insurmountable, entrepreneurship without capital offers a refreshing alternative, demonstrating that creativity and innovation are often more valuable than substantial start-up capital.

One of the main characteristics of entrepreneurship without capital is the utilisation of existing resources and networks. Another key aspect of this entrepreneurship is flexibility and the ability to react quickly to changes in the market or industry. Without the burden of heavy financial commitments, entrepreneurs can easily adapt their business models and find innovative solutions to problems they face.

At its core, however, it is of course about the business idea itself.

The potential of business ideas that can be realised with little to no capital is enormous. Many successful start-ups began with nothing more than an idea and the determination to realise it. Examples such as Airbnb and Dropbox, which originally started with minimal resources, illustrate how companies with creative solutions and a strong focus on customer benefit can achieve global success. Such examples serve as inspiration for budding entrepreneurs and show that a lack of capital does not have to be an obstacle to success.

This book is part of a series, Volume 1 of which is mainly concerned with new and innovative tools for validating a business idea, and which analyses the following issues in depth:

- The use of big data and AI-supported analysis tools. These technologies make it possible to collect and analyse large amounts of data from various sources in order to identify consumer trends, unmet needs and emerging market niches.
- Furthermore, the lean startup method, which has gained popularity in recent years, has revolutionised the way business ideas are developed and tested. Instead of developing a fully developed business idea before launching it on the market, this approach encourages starting with a minimal product and continuously improving it based on user feedback.
- Another progressive approach is the use of crowdsourcing platforms and social media analytics. These make it possible to present ideas and concepts to a broad public and receive direct feedback, suggestions and even support from potential customers or users.
- The inclusion of virtual reality and augmented reality in the ideation process is another cutting-edge innovation that is still underutilised. These technologies can be used for prototyping and simulations to provide a realistic picture of how a product or service would work in the real world.

A key aspect of such business ideas is their inclusivity. They enable people from a wide range of backgrounds, including those with limited resources, to become entrepreneurs. This helps to create a more diverse economic landscape where unique and innovative solutions can emerge from different perspectives. This diversity of perspectives is critical to innovation as it helps to identify and address unmet needs that may be overlooked by more traditional businesses.

The business idea

Successful business ideas that require little to no capital are worth their weight in gold.

They often use digital technologies and platforms to develop, market and distribute products or services. This approach utilises the far-reaching possibilities of the internet and social media to gain access to global markets, create customer proximity and promote viral marketing. Such technologies allow entrepreneurs to experiment with minimal upfront costs, iterate quickly and adapt their business models based on customer feedback. This reduces the risk traditionally associated with starting a new business.

The potential of these business ideas also lies in their ability to scale quickly. Without the need for significant initial investment, entrepreneurs can focus their resources on developing their core product or service, creating a strong foundation for future growth. This lean model enables efficient utilisation of capital and resources, allowing companies to respond and grow faster to market opportunities.

In addition, business ideas with low capital requirements often promote a culture of innovation and continuous learning. As the barriers to entry are lower, it encourages entrepreneurs to be creative, take risks and learn from mistakes. This mentality is crucial for the long-term sustainability and success of a company, as it leads to the development of robust and adaptable business models.

Business concepts that require little or no start-up capital are particularly attractive to founders who want to realise big entrepreneurial dreams with limited financial resources. The secret of their success often lies in the clever utilisation of their own skills, the strategic use of online platforms and the establishment of a strong presence in the digital space. By prioritising creativity and innovative approaches over the need for a large start-up budget, they open up numerous paths to business success.

Notable examples of ventures that have become global phenomena with minimal initial investment include not only Dropbox and Airbnb, but also the likes of:

- **Instagram**: Originally started as a simple photo-sharing app by Kevin Systrom and Mike Krieger. The founders used their programming skills to create a platform that allowed users to share and comment on photos. With minimal initial investment, mainly in servers and development, Instagram grew quickly and was eventually bought by Facebook for one billion US dollars.
- **Slack**: Stewart Butterfield originally founded Slack as an internal communication tool for his former company, which was working on an online game. The project for the game fell through, but Slack proved so useful that it became a product in its own right. With low initial costs for developing and hosting the platform, Slack became one of the fastest growing business applications of all time.
- **Mailchimp**: Started as a side project by Ben Chestnut and Dan Kurzius, Mailchimp developed into a leading email marketing tool for small and medium-sized companies. With a strong focus on usability and customer needs, Mailchimp required little start-up capital as it was initially launched as a service for existing

customers before being developed into a standalone product.

- **GitHub**: This company started as a platform for software developers to share and collaborate on code. Founded by Tom Preston-Werner, Chris Wanstrath and PJ Hyett, GitHub initially only required the technical expertise of its founders and a simple web infrastructure. Without much initial investment, it developed into an indispensable tool for developers worldwide and was eventually acquired by Microsoft for USD 7.5 billion.
- **Canva**: Melanie Perkins, Cliff Obrecht and Cameron Adams founded Canva with the vision of making design accessible to everyone. Originally conceived as an educational tool, Canva needed little more than the creativity and determination of its founders to build a user-friendly design platform. Today, Canva is worth billions and enables users without professional design skills to create stunning graphics.
- **Etsy**: The online marketplace for handmade and vintage items was founded by Rob Kalin, Chris Maguire and Haim Schoppik. Etsy began as a simple website that allowed small makers to offer their goods to a global audience. With little initial cost to develop the site, Etsy has grown into a leading online marketplace offering unique products to both buyers and sellers.
- **WhatsApp**: Brian Acton and Jan Koum, the founders of WhatsApp, launched the messaging app with the aim of offering a fast, simple and inexpensive alternative to text messaging. With minimal investment in the development of the app, WhatsApp was able to grow quickly by focussing on simplicity, reliability and data protection. Eventually, WhatsApp was

bought by Facebook for around 19 billion US dollars, making it one of the biggest deals in tech history.

These examples show that with a strong vision, commitment and the skilful use of available resources, entrepreneurs can build successful businesses even without significant start-up capital. The key often lies in solving a specific problem or meeting an unmet need, coupled with the ability to scale quickly and adapt to the market.

The landscape of entrepreneurship is undergoing a remarkable transformation today, fuelled by rapid technological advances and the proliferation of digital platforms. These changes are opening up new opportunities for entrepreneurs and revolutionising traditional business models in ways that were unimaginable just a few decades ago.

Technological advances, particularly in areas such as artificial intelligence, blockchain, the Internet of Things and machine learning, have laid the foundation for a new era of entrepreneurship. These technologies provide entrepreneurs with powerful tools to develop innovative solutions that address complex problems in a wide range of industries.

Digital platforms play a crucial role in this changing landscape by significantly reducing the barriers to market entry. Platforms such as social media, e-commerce websites and app stores offer entrepreneurs immediate access to global markets and a broad customer base. These platforms allow small start-ups to showcase their products and services alongside established businesses, creating a more level playing field. They also foster a culture of collaboration and sharing by bringing together networks and communities of like-minded people who can share resources, exchange knowledge and collaboratively drive innovative projects forward.

Another key element of the new entrepreneurial landscape is the ability to scale quickly. Digital business models, especially those based on software or platform services, can often be expanded quickly at low marginal cost. This means that successful products or services can be rapidly scaled globally, leading to exponential growth and the ability to quickly capture market share.

Digitalisation has also led to a change in the way companies interact with their customers and create value. Customer experiences are increasingly personalised, with companies using data and analytics to offer tailored services and products. This customer-centric approach strengthens customer loyalty and opens up new revenue streams through data-driven insights.

Strategies for identifying niche markets and unmet needs.

The examples of successful start-ups mentioned at the beginning show that gaps in the market were often recognised and served with the new business idea. Identifying and evaluating niche markets and recognising unmet needs are crucial steps in founding a successful business, especially when there is little capital available. A well-defined niche allows you to focus on a specific target audience and offer customised solutions that stand out from the crowd. Here are some strategies to help recognise and evaluate such opportunities:

Conduct market research

Researching and understanding market trends, industry developments and consumer preferences are fundamental steps on the road to a successful business start-up, especially when working with limited financial resources. Comprehensive market research is essential to gain solid insights into the target market. This process often begins with the use of digital resources and analytical tools that provide an overview of current and emerging trends.

By delving deep into online resources, relevant industry publications and specialised market research reports, you can gain a nuanced understanding of the market. It's important to look out for signals of areas of consistent growth where competition is not yet oversaturated. This opens up opportunities to occupy a niche that may have been overlooked by existing market players.

Tools such as Google Trends provide an initial indication of interest in certain topics or products over time. More advanced databases such as Statista or IBISWorld provide more in-depth analyses of industry trends, market volumes and growth expectations. Using these tools enables entrepreneurs to make data-driven decisions and identify areas where there is or is likely to be unmet demand.

This first phase of market exploration is important to lay a solid foundation for further business planning. It not only helps to identify potential gaps in the market, but also to better assess the risks and challenges that could be associated with launching a new product or service. Armed with these insights, founders can then develop more targeted strategies to successfully establish their business ideas on the market, even if they are working with limited initial investment.

Utilising customer feedback and social media

Thoroughly analysing social media and customer reviews is an extremely effective method of gaining in-depth insights into the wishes and needs of the target group. These platforms act as direct communication channels where users openly share their experiences, needs and frustrations. By carefully observing and analysing these discussions, entrepreneurs can gain valuable information that is essential for identifying unfulfilled market niches and developing targeted solutions.

Social networks such as X, Facebook and Reddit, as well as industry-specific forums, provide a rich source of data on moods and opinions. Users share their experiences with products or services and express their unmet needs. The challenge is to filter out the relevant insights from the wealth of information. This requires a systematic approach: Look for patterns and recurring themes that point to specific problems or wishes that are not yet addressed by existing offerings.

This approach makes it possible to learn directly from the consumer's perspective and place their needs at the centre of product or service development. Another advantage of this method is the ability to react quickly to changing market conditions or consumer preferences. In an environment where customer expectations are constantly evolving, the agile integration of user feedback into the development process offers a decisive competitive advantage.

Various data analysis tools and techniques can be used to draw meaningful insights from this unstructured data. Sentiment analyses, keyword tracking and the monitoring of specific topics or complaints are just some of the methods that can be used to identify relevant trends and needs. Such findings form a solid basis for the development of innovative solutions that are precisely tailored to the needs of the target group and effectively occupy unfulfilled market niches.

Carry out a competitive analysis

Conducting a competitive analysis is a crucial step in gaining an in-depth understanding of the market and identifying potential gaps in competitors' offerings. By taking a close look at competitors' product variety, customer service, marketing strategies and customer feedback, insights can be gained that reveal where customers' needs may not be fully met. This analysis makes it possible to discover areas where there are opportunities to differentiate or occupy a niche.

A careful examination of the competitors' product range and services can reveal where there is room for improvement or what innovative approaches are available to set the company apart from the market. It is important to recognise not only the strengths but also the weaknesses of competitors in order to develop strategic advantages.

Analysing customer service provides insights into customer satisfaction and areas where there may be frustrations or complaints. Important lessons can be learned from this and measures can be derived to optimise your own customer service and thus create added value compared to the competition.

Studying competitors' marketing strategies can also be informative to understand how they address their target group and which channels or messages they use. This can help to refine your own marketing approaches and identify potentially neglected segments or unutilised communication channels.

Customer feedback - whether through direct reviews, social media or customer service enquiries - provides a direct source to understand the strengths and weaknesses of competitors from the customer's perspective. This information is invaluable for better tailoring your own offering to the needs and wishes of your target group.

The SWOT analysis is a tried and tested tool for evaluating the findings in a structured manner. It helps to systematically record and compare the strengths, weaknesses, opportunities and threats of both your own business model and that of your competitors. This analysis enables well-founded business decisions to be made in order to successfully position oneself in the market and to specifically address the segments neglected by current providers.

Develop prototypes and MVPs

Developing a prototype or minimum viable product (MVP) is a strategic method for efficiently testing and further developing a business idea with limited resources. This approach makes it possible to turn a basic framework of the idea into reality in order to gather practical user feedback at an early stage. The main objective is to provide the core functionalities necessary to fulfil the basic needs of the target group while keeping effort and costs as low as possible.

The value of such an approach lies in the direct interaction with the first users. Their feedback is invaluable in gaining insights into how the product or service works in real-world use and where adjustments or improvements are needed. This feedback serves as a guide for iterations and improvements that better customise the offering to the customer's needs and wishes.

By starting with an MVP, you can reduce the risk normally associated with large initial investments. It allows entrepreneurs to validate market acceptance and interest in their idea before investing significant sums in product development or scaling. Such an iterative process helps to avoid wrong decisions and unnecessary expenditure by focussing on the essentials and responding flexibly to user feedback.

This practical approach promotes rapid learning and adaptation, which is particularly important in the early phases of business development. By focussing on an MVP, entrepreneurs can get to market faster, collect user data and effectively test product-market fit. The insights gained from this are fundamental to further developing the product or service and creating a solid foundation for future investment and growth.

Networking and industry events

Actively participating in industry events and immersing yourself in professional networks play a pivotal role in building a successful business, especially when starting out with limited resources. Not only do these interactions provide the opportunity to gain direct feedback and deeper insights into the specific challenges and unmet needs within your target industry, but they also open up access to a wealth of resources and knowledge that would be difficult to tap into otherwise.

By interacting with like-minded people and established players in the industry, you can gain valuable perspectives that will sharpen your view of the market and inspire new ideas for products or services. Such contacts can shed light on niche markets that have previously been overlooked or where there is a visible need that has not yet been adequately addressed. These insights are often crucial to shaping your offering so that it stands out from the competition and offers real added value for your target customers.

Networking also offers the opportunity to build relationships with potential customers, business partners or investors. These connections can prove invaluable when it comes to raising seed capital, accessing distribution channels or expanding your customer base. Equally valuable is the opportunity to find mentors whose experience and guidance can help you avoid common pitfalls and accelerate the development of your business.

In addition, involvement in professional networks and industry associations can lead to partnerships that can be essential for scaling your business model. Co-operations with other companies or specialists offer the opportunity to utilise synergies and jointly develop markets that would be too complex or cost-intensive to go it alone.

Consciously maintaining these networks and ongoing dialogue with industry peers are therefore fundamental building blocks for building a robust business foundation. This strategy not only allows you to develop a deep understanding of the dynamics of your target market, but also ensures you have access to resources, knowledge and support that can be critical to the success of your business.

Agile development and customisation

Be ready to adapt your strategy based on the feedback you receive and the data you collect. An agile approach allows you to react quickly to changes in the market or in customer preferences. This flexibility is particularly important in niche markets where customer needs can be specific and dynamic.

By applying these strategies, you can not only identify niche markets and unmet needs, but also assess how well you can respond to them with your resources, capabilities and business model. A deep understanding of your target market and the ability to respond quickly and cost-effectively to insights are critical to success, especially when available capital is limited.

100 business ideas explained

Developing innovative business ideas that are suitable for start-ups with little or no start-up capital is a challenge that requires creativity and a deep insight into current and future market trends. Indeed, the spectrum of such business ideas is broad and includes both simple and highly complex concepts. To ensure a broad overview, we look at different areas of the economy, ranging from educational services such as tutoring to advanced technologies such as AI-based applications.

Services in the IT sector

Start-ups in the IT sector are particularly common due to several key factors. Firstly, the digital transformation has become a key driver of economic and social developments in all areas of life. Businesses and consumers are increasingly reliant on digital technologies to increase efficiency, open up new markets and meet the demands of modern life. This ubiquitous demand for IT solutions creates a fertile foundation for new companies offering innovative products and services.

Secondly, start-ups in the IT sector often require less capital to get started compared to traditional industries. Software-based businesses can start with minimal physical resources, as their main investment is usually in the development of software and digital platforms. The ability to start a business with low initial investment makes the IT sector attractive to individuals and small teams who have innovative ideas but do not have extensive financial resources.

Thirdly, the scalability and global reach of digital products enable IT start-ups to grow quickly and tap into markets far beyond their geographical locations. A successful digital product or service can be delivered to a large number of users worldwide with relatively little additional effort. This scalability attracts entrepreneurs looking for opportunities to make a significant impact and expand quickly.

Fourthly, the IT sector offers a dynamic and constantly evolving environment in which technological advances open up new business opportunities. The rapid development of new technologies such as artificial intelligence, blockchain, cloud computing and the Internet of Things is constantly creating new niches and use cases that require innovative solutions. Entrepreneurs in the IT sector are in a good position to capitalise on these trends by adapting quickly and developing products that match the latest technological possibilities.

Finally, the culture of innovation and entrepreneurship in the IT sector has created a supportive community of investors, mentors and like-minded individuals who support start-ups through funding, advice and networking opportunities. These ecosystems, often centred in technology hubs and incubators, provide valuable resources and access to knowledge that is critical to the success of young companies.

IT support and consulting

Starting an IT support and consultancy service can be an excellent business opportunity, especially at a time when reliance on technology is continually growing in both professional and personal spheres. Companies, small business owners and individuals are often looking for reliable, expert support to help them overcome their technology challenges. This ranges from setting up and maintaining their IT infrastructure to solving specific software problems or implementing cyber security measures.

Fundamentals

A key to success in this field is to have a deep understanding of the current IT landscape and current technologies. This includes knowledge of network technologies, operating systems, cloud services, cyber security and data management. As technology is rapidly evolving, it is equally important to continuously learn and stay up to date with the latest technological developments and best practices.

Another key component is building strong customer relationships. Trust and reliability are crucial when it comes to establishing long-term partnerships with customers. An effective IT support and consultancy service listens to the needs of its customers, provides customised solutions and responds promptly and efficiently to requests or problems. The ability to translate complex technical concepts into easy-to-understand language can also help to increase customer trust and satisfaction.

Marketing and networking are crucial to publicising your business and attracting customers. Digital marketing, including a professional website, search engine optimisation (SEO) and social media presence, can be effective in promoting your services and building an online community. At the same time, local networking events, trade conferences and industry association memberships can provide valuable opportunities to make contacts and establish partnerships.

In the early stages, it can be helpful to focus on a niche or specialised services to differentiate yourself from the competition. This could include specialising in certain technologies, industries or service packages that are tailored to the specific needs of small businesses or certain market segments.

Setting up an IT support and consulting service not only opens up opportunities, but also brings challenges that need to be overcome. One important aspect of this is setting yourself apart from the competition. In a market that appears increasingly saturated, it is crucial to develop a unique selling point. This can be done by specialising in certain technologies, sectors or by offering unique service packages. For example, an IT support company could specialise in providing services to the healthcare sector by familiarising itself with the specific requirements and regulations of this industry.

Another important step is certification and further training. Certificates from recognised institutions can strengthen credibility and trust in your company's expertise. They signal to customers that you and your team are at the cutting edge of technology and follow best practices. In addition, offering training courses or workshops to customers can be an additional source of revenue while strengthening the bond with your customers.

Technology is constantly evolving, and IT support and consulting organisations need to stay proactive to understand the latest trends and threats. This means staying on top of developments in areas such as artificial intelligence, machine learning, the Internet of Things (IoT) and cybersecurity. A deep understanding of these areas makes it possible to plan ahead and offer customers innovative solutions that give them a competitive edge.

In addition to technical expertise, it is important to establish effective customer relationship management (CRM). A CRM system can help to manage customer interactions, process service requests efficiently and offer personalised services. This not only improves customer satisfaction, but also enables the collection of valuable data on customer needs and preferences that can be used for further business development.

A strong online presence is essential to be successful in today's digital world. In addition to a professional website and active social media participation, content marketing can be an effective strategy. By sharing high-quality, informative content that reflects your company's expertise, you can increase visibility, position yourself as a thought leader in your industry and generate organic traffic.

Finally, it is important to offer flexible and scalable services that adapt to the changing needs of customers. This could mean developing packages that are suitable for different customer segments, from start-ups to established companies. By combining flexibility in service offerings with a strong focus on customer service and continuous training, you position your company as a reliable partner in the IT industry.

Possible specialisations for newcomers

The IT industry offers a variety of niches and sub-areas in which an IT support and consulting service can specialise. These specialisations make it possible to stand out from the competition and address specific customer needs. Here are some areas in which specialisation can be particularly promising:

- **Cyber security:** With the increasing threat of cyber attacks, services that focus on improving the security of

information systems can be in high demand. These include penetration testing, security audits, security policy development, incident response and advice on data protection compliance.
- **Cloud services**: With the growing popularity of cloud solutions, there is an increasing need for advice and support on migrating to the cloud, cloud management and optimising cloud infrastructures. Expertise in specific cloud platforms such as AWS, Google Cloud or Microsoft Azure can be particularly valuable here.
- **Data management and analytics**: Companies are collecting more and more data, but are often faced with the challenge of utilising it effectively. Specialists in the field of data management and analytics can provide support with data integration, processing, analysis and the implementation of business intelligence solutions.
- **Network management**: The planning, implementation and maintenance of company networks is a critical IT area. Specialisations can include network design, performance optimisation, WLAN services or the implementation of software-defined networking (SDN).
- **Compliance and IT governance**: Many industries are subject to strict regulatory requirements regarding the handling of data and IT security. Expertise in specific legal frameworks (e.g. GDPR, HIPAA) and in advising on compliance issues can enable high-quality consulting services.
- **Specialised industry solutions**: Specialising in IT solutions for specific industries (e.g. healthcare, financial services, retail, manufacturing) enables in-depth

knowledge of the respective requirements and challenges and provides the opportunity to offer customised services.
- **Software development and maintenance**: Providing bespoke software development, including app development, legacy system modernisation and maintenance of existing applications, can be a lucrative niche.
- **Digital transformation**: Advice on digital transformation, including the introduction of digital technologies into business processes and the digital reorientation of companies, is a growing area that helps companies to remain competitive in the digital era.
- **Internet of Things (IoT):** With the increasing spread of IoT devices in industry and private households, new business opportunities are emerging in areas such as IoT security, network integration and data analysis.
- **Artificial intelligence and machine learning**: Companies that offer consulting and implementation services in the fields of AI and machine learning can benefit from the increasing demand for intelligent automation and decision support systems.

By focussing on one or more of these niches, an IT support and consulting service can not only deepen its expertise, but also strengthen its market position and establish itself as a valuable partner for its customers.

Artificial intelligence and machine learning

Specialising in artificial intelligence (AI) and machine learning (ML) as a start-up offers enormous potential to develop innovative solutions and consulting services that help companies automate and optimise their processes. These technologies have the potential to transform almost every aspect of business, from customer interaction to product development and decision-making. Here are some approaches you can take as a start-up in this area:

Development of customised AI solutions

The development of customised AI solutions opens up a wide range of opportunities for companies that want to increase their efficiency, improve customer satisfaction and offer innovative products and services. In this context, intelligent systems that are able to learn from large amounts of data, recognise patterns and make predictions based on them play a central role. Such an approach makes it possible to respond to the specific needs and challenges of each company individually.

One area in which customised AI solutions are particularly valuable is e-commerce. Here, personalised recommendation systems can be used to personalise the customer's shopping experience. These systems analyse the purchasing behaviour and preferences of users in order to make individually tailored product suggestions, which not only increases customer satisfaction but can also boost sales figures.

Another example is the automation of customer service through intelligent chatbots or voice assistants. These can process customer enquiries around the clock, which leads to faster and more efficient processing of requests and at the same time reduces the workload of the human customer service team. Such systems are constantly learning, improving their responses and becoming more effective over time.

In addition, advanced analytical methods can be used in the financial sector to recognise trends and patterns from historical data. This can be used for risk assessment, fraud detection or for predicting market developments. By analysing large amounts of data, AI models can provide insights that would not be possible with conventional methods and thus provide decision-makers with valuable information.

AI-supported process automation

The automation of routine processes through the use of artificial intelligence represents an attractive opportunity for start-ups to increase efficiency and reduce costs. By implementing AI systems, companies can relieve themselves of repetitive and time-consuming tasks and instead focus on strategic and creative aspects of their business activities.

A key area of application for AI-supported automation is customer service. Chatbots and virtual assistants can be used here to process customer enquiries automatically. These technologies are able to recognise and respond to a wide range of customer concerns, resulting in faster response times and greater customer satisfaction. At the same time, they free up the customer service team to focus on more complex enquiries. The continuous improvement of AI algorithms ensures that these systems become more accurate and helpful over time.

Another area in which AI-supported process automation offers major benefits is the optimisation of stock levels and supply chains. By using predictive analytics, companies can better predict future trends and fluctuations in demand and adjust their stocks accordingly. This leads to more efficient warehousing, reduces excess stock and minimises the risk of stock-outs at the same time. In addition, automation can help to streamline the supply chain and shorten delivery times by identifying optimal routes and delivery methods.

Automation also extends to the area of invoicing and accounting processes. AI-supported systems can automatically process invoices, reconcile payments and generate financial reports. This not only saves time, but also increases the accuracy of financial data by reducing human error. In addition, the automation of accounting processes enables real-time insight into the company's financial situation, which supports better decision-making.

AI-supported process automation therefore offers start-ups a way to make their companies efficient and competitive right from the start. By reducing manual tasks, founders and their teams can focus on the core aspects of their business and drive innovation. At the same time, automation helps to reduce operating costs and improve service quality, which overall boosts the company's competitiveness and growth.

Consultancy and strategy development

The role of a consultant in the field of artificial intelligence and machine learning opens up a multifaceted opportunity for start-ups to accompany and support companies on their path to digital transformation. This field of activity requires not only in-depth technical knowledge, but also the ability to translate complex technologies into strategic advantages. Experts in this field are in demand to shed light on the often complex field of AI and ML and to demonstrate its potential for companies of all sizes and from a wide range of industries.

The work primarily involves helping organisations to develop and implement strategies that enable them to benefit from the latest developments in AI and ML. This starts with basic education about what AI and ML can do, through to identifying specific use cases that will add real value to the organisation. Consultancy can help reduce uncertainty and define a clear direction for digital transformation.

An important aspect of the consultancy work is the assessment of the company's existing data infrastructure and technology landscape. By analysing existing systems and processes, consultants can make recommendations for improvements needed to lay the foundations for successful AI and ML applications. This can range from improving data quality and accessibility to implementing advanced data analytics platforms.

In addition, staff training and development play a key role. The introduction of AI and ML technologies often requires new skills and knowledge, both for IT professionals and for employees who come into contact with these technologies in their day-to-day work. Through targeted training programmes, consultants can help raise awareness and understanding of AI and ML within the company and ensure that all employees are able to work effectively with the new technologies.

Consulting in the field of AI and ML is therefore not just a question of technical implementation, but also a process of organisational change. By combining technical expertise, strategic planning and change management, consultants can help companies overcome the challenges of digital transformation and fully utilise the benefits of AI and ML. In this dynamic and fast-moving field, start-ups that specialise as consultants can play a key role in shaping the future of companies and industries.

Development and implementation of AI-supported products

The development and implementation of AI-supported products represents enormous potential for start-ups to bring innovative solutions to the market that can permanently change everyday life and business processes. At the centre of these ventures is the creative application of artificial intelligence and machine learning to create products that can act intelligently, networked and increasingly autonomously. These products range from applications that transform the smartphone into a personal assistant, to devices that revolutionise health monitoring, to security systems that use facial recognition technology to provide protection and security.

A key aspect in the development of AI-supported products is a deep understanding of the needs and challenges that users face in their everyday lives or that companies face in their specific industries. This knowledge makes it possible to design targeted solutions that address real problems and offer significant added value. The ability to implement AI and ML in such a way that they can be seamlessly integrated into people's lives and companies' processes is crucial.

The development of intelligent smartphone applications, for example, opens up a wide range of possibilities, from personalised learning aids to advanced fitness and health trackers that analyse user behaviour and provide customised recommendations. The challenge here lies in creating intuitive user interfaces and ensuring that the application provides real benefits that go beyond the capabilities of conventional apps.

In the field of health monitoring, AI-supported devices offer the opportunity to detect warning signals at an early stage and recommend preventive measures by continuously collecting and analysing health data. The development of such products requires not only technical expertise, but also a deep understanding of medical needs and regulatory requirements.

Security systems based on facial recognition technology are again an innovative solution to increase the security of buildings and public spaces. However, these systems need to be carefully developed to address privacy concerns and optimise the accuracy of recognition to minimise false alarms and ensure user acceptance.

For start-ups in the field of AI-supported product development, it is essential to constantly educate themselves and keep their finger on the pulse of technological development in order to fully utilise the possibilities of AI and ML. At the same time, it is important to maintain partnerships with experts from the target industries to ensure that the products developed are not only technologically advanced, but also practically applicable and ready for the market. The path from idea to successful product requires patience, perseverance and a willingness to continuously learn and adapt. However, the prospect of making a real difference with an AI-supported product offers an inspiring vision for motivated start-ups.

Data protection and ethical counselling

In today's world, where artificial intelligence is increasingly moving to the centre of business and social processes, data protection and ethical considerations are becoming more and more important. Start-ups that specialise in providing services in this area are addressing a critical need for modern companies: the responsible use of AI technologies.

Developing ethical guidelines for the use of AI is a complex endeavour that requires a deep understanding of both the technological aspects and the potential social impact. Consultants in this field work closely with organisations to develop policies that not only harness the innovative potential of AI, but also ensure that these technologies are used in accordance with ethical principles and societal values.

A key concern here is to ensure that AI systems are free from bias. Given that AI models learn from the data used to train them, there is a risk that existing biases will feed into the algorithms, producing decisions that penalise certain groups. Consultants work at the intersection of technology and social justice by developing strategies to verify and improve the fairness and impartiality of AI systems.

In addition, compliance with data protection laws is a critical element in dealing with AI. With the growing sensitivity to data protection issues and the entry into force of strict laws such as the European General Data Protection Regulation (GDPR), organisations need to ensure that their AI applications respect user privacy and comply with legal requirements. Consultancy services in this area include assessing AI systems for compliance, advising on the implementation of data protection measures and training employees in data protection-related topics.

For start-ups wishing to establish themselves in this field, a multi-layered field of activity is opening up that combines technical expertise with legal and ethical skills. The challenge is not only to help companies navigate the complex web of legal requirements, but also to design and utilise AI responsibly. This requires constant engagement with the latest developments in AI technology, in-depth knowledge of the relevant legal situation and the ability to translate ethical principles into practical corporate strategies.

For start-ups involved in this area, there is an opportunity to be at the forefront of a movement that aims to utilise technology responsibly and sustainably.

Success factors

It is important to note that the successful use of AI and ML in companies requires not only technical skills, but also an understanding of customers' specific business processes and challenges. Successful AI solutions are often the result of close collaboration between technology experts and business leaders.

You should also constantly educate yourself and keep up to date, as the technologies and methods in AI and ML are evolving rapidly. Networking with other professionals in the field, attending conferences and participating in professional groups can help you keep your knowledge up to date and identify new business opportunities.

Social Media Management

The importance of social media for companies of all sizes can hardly be overestimated, as it now plays a central role in the modern business world. It provides a platform for branding, customer communication and direct sales. For start-ups with knowledge of social media marketing, this opens up a promising field of activity as a social media manager. This role involves much more than simply managing social media profiles. It is about developing a comprehensive strategy that supports the company's goals, be it by increasing brand awareness, engagement or direct sales generation.

A social media manager helps to shape and maintain a company's online presence. This includes planning, creating and publishing content across different platforms. Each platform has its own user base and requires a customised approach, be it Instagram, Facebook, Twitter, LinkedIn or TikTok. The ability to understand the tone and style of each channel and adapt content accordingly is crucial. It also involves analysing performance data to evaluate and adjust the effectiveness of the social media strategy. This requires a good understanding of analytics tools and metrics such as reach, engagement and conversion.

Another important aspect is community management, i.e. building and maintaining relationships with followers and customers via social media. This includes responding to enquiries, moderating discussions and actively engaging with the community to create a positive and interactive brand experience.

For start-ups in the field of social media management, it is important to keep up to date with the rapidly changing trends and algorithms of the various platforms. Social media is a dynamic field, and what works today may be outdated tomorrow. Continuous training and adaptability are therefore essential.

In addition, it is beneficial to have knowledge in related fields such as graphic design, video production or copywriting, as high-quality, engaging content is crucial for success on social media. The ability to produce creative and compelling content that reflects the brand identity while appealing to the target audience is a key to success.

The demand for qualified social media managers is high, especially among small and medium-sized companies that often do not have the resources to fill this role internally. For start-ups, this is an opportunity to fill an important gap while capitalising on the growing importance of digital presence in the business world. Through a combination of strategic planning, creative content creation and effective community management, they can help companies achieve their goals on social media and successfully position their brand. A tip: look for companies with a poor social media presence and develop a concept without being asked. Presenting this is often easier than presenting yourself.

Webinar and online course production

The demand for online education and training has increased significantly in recent years, making the production and marketing of webinars and online courses a lucrative field for start-ups. This field of activity opens up the possibility of helping experts and professionals from various sectors to make their knowledge accessible to a wider audience. The role of such a service provider is multi-faceted and includes technical support, content development and the planning and implementation of marketing strategies.

Technical support is a fundamental aspect of this business model. While many experts have extensive expertise, they have limited knowledge of the technical aspects of online course production. This is where start-ups can come in by offering solutions for the recording, editing and delivery of video material. This includes choosing the right software and hardware, setting up recording studios and editing videos to ensure a professional end product. In addition, technical support in setting up and managing learning management systems (LMS) used to deliver online courses and webinars is crucial.

Content development is another important area. This includes support in structuring the course, creating curricula and developing supporting materials such as presentations, worksheets and tests. The challenge is to make the material not only informative, but also interactive and engaging in order to motivate participants and maximise learning success.

Added to this is the importance of effective marketing strategies to reach the target group and encourage participation. This includes optimising online presence through search engine optimisation (SEO), using social media to promote courses and webinars, email marketing campaigns and, where appropriate, paid advertising. A deep understanding of the target audience and the use of appropriate marketing channels are key to increasing the visibility and attractiveness of the courses on offer.

For start-ups in this field, it is important to have a broad range of skills or to form a team that combines technical expertise, pedagogical competence and marketing skills. The ability to work closely with experts and translate their visions into effective learning programmes is the key to success. In addition, flexibility is required to respond to the specific needs and requirements of different specialisms.

With the growing market for online education, the production and marketing of webinars and online courses offers an excellent opportunity for start-ups to establish themselves in a promising and dynamic field. By providing high quality services, they can not only help professionals to share their knowledge, but also make a valuable contribution to education and training.

Podcast production and consulting

The growing popularity of podcasts has opened up a new dimension in the world of digital media and entertainment. With millions of listeners worldwide, podcasts provide a unique platform for stories, expertise and discussion on a wide range of topics. For start-ups with expertise in audio production, content development and marketing, podcast production and consultancy offers a promising field of activity.

The technical production of podcasts is at the centre of this business area. This includes the provision of services such as recording, editing and audio mastering to produce high quality podcast episodes. Technical support can also include selecting and setting up the right audio equipment for clients, from microphones to mixing consoles and recording software. The ability to deliver clean, well-mixed sound is critical to the success of a podcast, as audio quality directly affects the listening experience.

In addition to technical production, content development plays a central role. Start-ups can offer support in the conception and structuring of podcast series, from the development of the overarching theme to the planning of individual episodes. This includes advice on selecting topics that are both relevant and appealing to the target audience, as well as support with scripting and designing interview questions. Well-thought-out content that adds value and appeals to the target audience is a key factor in audience retention and growth.

In addition, the marketing of podcasts is a crucial aspect of reaching and retaining a wide audience. Services in this area can include the development and implementation of marketing strategies aimed at promoting the podcast through various channels. This includes social media marketing, search engine optimisation for podcasts, placing advertisements on other podcasts and networking with other podcasters and media platforms. Effective marketing helps to increase the visibility of the podcast and build a loyal listener base.

For podcast production and consulting start-ups, it is important to have a deep understanding of the podcast landscape and the technical aspects of audio production. At the same time, they must be able to provide creative and strategic content and marketing solutions that meet the needs and goals of their clients. The ability to work closely with clients and provide customised solutions that highlight their unique voice and message is critical to success in this field.

With the growing demand for podcast content and the constant search by content creators for high quality production and strategic advice, podcast production and consultancy offers an exciting opportunity for start-ups to establish themselves in a dynamic and creative field.

SEO consulting

Optimising a company's online presence through search engine optimisation (SEO) has become essential in today's digitalised world. As more and more companies recognise the value of a strong online presence, the demand for professionals who are able to improve the visibility and ranking of websites in search engines is growing. For start-ups with expertise in SEO, this is an excellent opportunity to become an SEO consultant and help companies achieve their digital marketing goals.

As SEO consultants, the focus is on developing customised strategies that are tailored to the specific needs and goals of each company. This begins with a comprehensive analysis of current website performance, including a review of content, website structure, usability and existing backlink profiles. Based on this analysis, optimisation measures are identified that aim to make the website more attractive to both search engines and users.

An essential part of SEO consulting is the development of an effective keyword strategy. This involves identifying relevant and powerful keywords that reflect the search behaviour of the target audience and form the basis for creating or optimising content. The optimisation of on-page elements such as titles, meta descriptions, header tags and internal links is also crucial to send relevant signals to search engines that can positively influence rankings.

In addition, SEO consulting includes advice on technical aspects of the website, such as loading speed, mobile-friendliness and the implementation of structured data. These technical optimisations are crucial to ensure that websites can be crawled and indexed efficiently by search engines and provide a positive user experience.

Another important area in which SEO consultants can support companies is the development and implementation of an effective content strategy. High quality, relevant and regularly updated content is a key element in attracting both users and search engines. SEO consultants work closely with companies to plan and produce content that not only targets keywords but also provides real value to the target audience.

In addition to optimising existing content and the technical infrastructure, link building is an important component of successful SEO strategies. SEO consultants develop strategies to generate high-quality backlinks from trusted websites, which is a key ranking factor. This can be achieved through content marketing, guest posts, partnerships and other methods.

For start-ups in the SEO consulting field, it's crucial to stay on top of the ever-evolving SEO practices and search engine algorithm updates. The ability to conduct data-driven analyses, develop creative solutions and work closely with clients to achieve their online marketing goals is key to success. Given the high demand for SEO expertise, SEO consulting offers an exciting opportunity for start-ups to establish themselves in a dynamic and high-growth field.

Digital art and design

The suitability of digital art and design for start-ups depends on various factors, including market needs, target group, the skills of the founder and technological development. Digital art and design covers a broad spectrum, ranging from graphic design to web design to the creation of digital artwork for online sale. These areas offer numerous opportunities to start a business, each with its own challenges and opportunities.

The market for digital art and design has grown exponentially in recent years, driven in part by the rise of social media, the increasing demand for online content and the development of new platforms for the sale and distribution of digital works. A key element for a successful start-up in this field is the ability to adapt quickly to new trends and technologies, such as the use of augmented reality and virtual reality for immersive design or the creation of NFTs (non-fungible tokens) for the digital art market.

A key advantage of digital art and design for start-ups is the relatively low barrier to entry compared to traditional business models. The basic requirements are often just a powerful computer, the appropriate software and a strong online presence. Social media and online platforms also offer low-cost opportunities to present works and reach a target group.

However, starting a business in the field of digital art and design also requires specific knowledge and skills, not only in the creative field, but also in terms of marketing, customer acquisition and retention, and business management. Success depends heavily on the ability to establish yourself as a brand, attract the attention of potential customers and stand out from the competition.

Networking and community engagement play a crucial role in success in the digital art and design industry. Participating in online forums, collaborating with other artists and designers and attending trade fairs and conferences can help you make contacts, strengthen your brand and generate new orders.

In financial terms, the sources of income can be diverse, from commissioned work to the sale of prints or digital downloads to income from online courses and tutorials for budding artists and designers. Diversifying revenue streams can help minimise financial risk and ensure a stable income.

Online community management

If you have experience in building and maintaining online communities, there are many opportunities for you to offer your services to companies that want to strengthen their presence on social networks. In today's digital world, a strong online presence is no longer just an add-on for companies, but a necessity. Social media plays a central role in this, as it allows you to communicate directly and personally with your target audience, create brand awareness and increase customer loyalty.

The ability to build an engaged community around a brand is a valuable skill. It requires a deep understanding of how digital platforms work, as well as knowledge of content creation, digital marketing, data analytics and customer service. Your services could include a range of tasks including:

- Strategy development: Creating a customised social media strategy that is aligned with the company's goals, whether it's to increase brand awareness, boost engagement or drive sales.
- Content creation and management: planning, creating and managing content that resonates and drives engagement. This includes not only writing copy and designing images, but also creating videos, podcasts and other interactive content formats.
- Community engagement: Active participation and moderation of discussions within the community, answering questions and comments, and managing feedback and complaints. This helps to create a positive and welcoming atmosphere and strengthen loyalty to the brand.
- Influencer marketing: Identification and collaboration with influencers who fit the brand in order to increase reach and strengthen trust in the brand through recommendations.
- Analysis and reporting: Monitoring key performance indicators (KPIs) and analysing data to measure the success of social media activities. Strategies can be adapted and optimised based on these analyses.

For companies looking to grow their online presence, it's crucial to find partners who not only bring technical expertise and creative skills, but also have a deep understanding of their brand and target audience. As an expert in building and maintaining online communities, you could offer valuable insights and strategies to help businesses become more visible and relevant in the digital landscape.

Before offering your services, it is important to carefully analyse and document your own experiences and successes. Create a portfolio that highlights your previous work, the communities you have built and the results you have achieved. This will not only show potential clients your expertise, but will also build confidence in your ability to achieve similar successes for their brand.

The demand for experts in social media and community management continues to grow as companies realise how important these elements are to their success. With the right skills and a clear understanding of how to position brands in the digital world, you can become a valuable resource for any organisation looking to strengthen its online presence.

Digital productivity consulting

Providing consultancy services on the use of digital tools and software to improve efficiency can be a highly valuable service for individuals and organisations looking to increase their productivity. In today's fast-paced business world, where efficiency and productivity are critical factors for success, the right digital tools can make a significant difference. As a consultant in this field, you could play a key role in helping clients optimise their workflows, save time and ultimately achieve their business goals more effectively.

Firstly, it is important to develop understanding and expertise in a wide range of digital tools and software solutions that are used in different business areas. These include project management tools, collaboration platforms, CRM (customer relationship management) systems, ERP (enterprise resource planning) systems, automation tools and data analysis software. You should not only understand how these tools work, but also how they can best be used in different business environments to optimise processes and increase productivity.

Your advisory services can take various forms, depending on the specific needs of your customers:

- Needs analysis: Firstly, you could conduct a thorough analysis of the current workflows, tools and technologies your client uses to identify areas for improvement.
- Customised solution development: Based on the analysis, you will develop customised solutions that are specifically tailored to the customer's needs and objectives. This could include the selection and implementation of new tools, the training of staff in their use or the optimisation of existing systems.
- Training and support: A key part of your service could be to provide training for individuals and teams to ensure they can use the selected tools effectively. In addition, you could offer ongoing support and advice to ensure sustainable use and adaptation to changing needs.
- Measuring success and optimisation: Finally, you could introduce methods to measure the improvements achieved through the implementation of

digital tools. This data can then be used to further refine strategies and continuously improve efficiency.

To attract clients to your consulting services, it is important to build a strong online presence and position yourself as an expert in your field. This can be done by publishing specialised articles, holding webinars, actively engaging on social media and networking at industry-related events. Recommendations from satisfied customers can also play an important role in generating new business.

As a consultant for digital tools and software to improve efficiency, you have the opportunity to make an impact on the way individuals and organisations work. By combining your technical knowledge with an understanding of business processes, you can provide customised solutions that deliver real improvements in productivity. With the right approach and commitment, you can build a successful consultancy business providing valuable services to clients who want to succeed in the digital economy.

Personalised gift design

Using your creative skills to create personalised gifts such as photo books, bespoke clothing or engraved jewellery is a great way to build a business selling online. Personalised products are very popular as they offer the opportunity to create unique and meaningful gifts tailored to the individual preferences and needs of the recipient. This market has developed considerably in recent years and offers numerous opportunities for creative entrepreneurs.

The first step is to develop your product line. This can include

- Photo books that capture special events such as weddings, birthdays or holidays.
- Customised clothing, including T-shirts, hats or bags with special designs, logos or texts.
- Engraved jewellery where customers can have names, dates or special messages incorporated into rings, pendants or bracelets.

When developing your products, it is important to focus on quality and offer services that allow customers to easily realise their own ideas. This includes using user-friendly design tools on your website or allowing customers to communicate directly with you for customised requests.

Once you have developed your products, the next step is to market and sell them. Social media and e-commerce platforms offer excellent channels for this.

- Social media such as Instagram, Facebook and Pinterest are ideal for showcasing your products and connecting with potential customers. By regularly posting attractive photos of your products, sharing customer feedback and interacting with your community, you can increase interest in your products and build a loyal following.
- E-commerce platforms such as Etsy, Shopify or Amazon Handmade offer a ready-made infrastructure for online sales. These platforms are specifically geared towards small businesses and artisans, making them ideal places to offer personalised gifts to a wide audience.

Successful marketing is the key to selling your personalised products. In addition to using social media, you should also consider other strategies such as:

- Email marketing to send offers, news or product design tips directly to your customers.
- Search engine optimisation (SEO) to improve the visibility of your website or online shop in search engine results.
- Use customer reviews and recommendations to build trust with new customers.

The ability to create unique and personalised experiences for your customers will not only help your product stand out from the crowd, but also build a loyal customer base that will come back to you time and time again. Success in this business requires creativity, a good understanding of your target audience and effective marketing strategies. With the right approach, you can build a thriving business that successfully sells personalised gifts through social media and e-commerce platforms.

Online music lessons

If you play an instrument or are talented in singing, you can offer online music lessons. This only requires your musical skills and a good internet connection.

Offering online music lessons is a great way to share your musical skills and knowledge while generating an income. At a time when digital platforms and the internet are playing an ever-increasing role in our daily lives, teaching music online opens up new ways to reach and teach students worldwide.

This model offers flexibility for both teachers and students and makes music education more accessible than ever before.

In order to offer online music lessons effectively, you need a few other basics in addition to your musical skills and a good internet connection:

- High-quality audio and video equipment: A good webcam and a high-quality microphone are crucial to ensure that your students can see and hear you and your instrument clearly. This significantly improves the quality of teaching.
- Quiet and well-lit classroom: Your classroom should be well-lit so that you are clearly visible in the video and free from background noise to minimise disruption during the lesson.
- Teaching materials and resources: Prepare teaching materials and resources that are specifically suitable for online teaching. These can include digital music sheets, recording software for exercises and interactive teaching aids.

There are various ways to market and offer your online music lessons:

- Own website or blog: Having your own website or blog can serve not only as a platform to offer your services, but also to demonstrate your expertise and commitment to music through blog posts, videos and student reviews.
- Social media: Use social media to promote your online music lessons. Platforms such as Instagram, Facebook and YouTube are great for giving insights

into your lessons, sharing free mini-lessons or performances and building a community.
- Online teaching platforms: There are specialised platforms such as TakeLessons, Lessonface and Tutorful that bring teachers and students together. These can be a valuable resource for attracting new students.

The design of your online lessons should be carefully planned to ensure an effective and engaging learning experience:

- Interactive and engaging lessons: Utilise technology and teaching strategies that make lessons interactive and engaging. This can include the use of music software, apps and interactive exercises.
- Customised lessons: Offer tailor-made lessons that are tailored to the individual needs and goals of your students. This increases student satisfaction and engagement.
- Feedback and progress assessment: Regular feedback is essential to assess your students' progress and help them improve. Use digital means to share recordings of exercises and provide feedback.

Offering online music lessons is not only a flexible and innovative way to share your musical talent and knowledge, but also offers the opportunity to reach a wide range of students and have a positive impact on their musical development. With the right equipment, effective marketing strategies and a well-thought-out teaching approach, you can build a successful online music teaching practice.

Remote tech support

Many people and small businesses need support with technical problems. If you have IT skills, you can offer a remote tech support service.

Offering remote tech support services is therefore a valuable business opportunity, especially at a time when technology has become essential for most people and small businesses. The increasing reliance on computers, smartphones and other technology in daily life and business operations is leading to a growing need for tech support. If you have IT skills, you can capitalise on this opportunity to offer services ranging from troubleshooting to setting up and maintaining systems.

As a remote tech support provider, you can offer a wide range of services including:

- Troubleshooting and technical support for software and hardware
- Installation and configuration of software applications
- Security checks and advice, including virus protection and malware removal
- Data backup and recovery services
- Advice and support in the selection and installation of new technologies
- Network setup and management, including Wi-Fi configuration
- Training and guidance on the use of various technologies and software

To successfully operate a remote tech support service, a few key components are required:

- Technical skills: A good understanding of computers, software, networks and security protocols is essential. Ongoing training is important to keep up with rapidly evolving technologies.
- Reliable technology: A stable and fast Internet connection as well as powerful computers and possibly special software for remote access to customer computers are required.
- Communication skills: The ability to explain complex technical concepts in a simple, understandable way is critical to success.
- Marketing: An effective marketing strategy that includes a professional website, social media presence and possibly local advertising will help you reach your target audience.
- Privacy and security: A strong commitment to privacy and security is essential to gaining the trust of your customers. This includes the use of secure remote access software and compliance with data protection regulations.
- Website: A professional website is crucial to showcase your services and provide potential customers with a first point of contact.
- Social media: An active presence on platforms such as LinkedIn, Facebook and Twitter can help to expand your network and promote your services.
- Referral programmes: Satisfied customers are often the best advertising media. A referral programme can encourage existing customers to recommend you to their friends and business partners.

- Local advertising: Although your service is remote, local advertising in community newspapers or on local online platforms can be helpful to create awareness in your community.
- Collaboration with local businesses: Forming partnerships with local businesses that offer complementary services can be a good way to attract customers.

Providing remote tech support can be a fulfilling and profitable endeavour if you have the right technical and business skills. The key to success lies in providing trustworthy, efficient and customer-centred services that meet the needs of your target audience. With the right approach and commitment, you can build a successful remote tech support business that provides valuable services to individuals and organisations.

Digital archive management

Help companies and individuals digitise and organise their documents, photos and other media for easier access and better preservation.

Offering services to digitise and organise documents, photos and other media is meeting a growing demand from both businesses and individuals. At a time when information management efficiency and data security are becoming increasingly important, digitisation offers an effective solution for improving access to information and preserving important documents and memories for the long term. By converting physical documents into digital formats, you can help your customers optimise their information flows, save space and improve the security of their data.

Services that you can offer are

- Digitisation of documents: Converting physical documents into digital formats. This includes letters, contracts, invoices, technical drawings and historical records.
- Digitisation of photos and videos: Scanning or digitising photographs, slides and negatives as well as converting analogue video formats into digital formats.
- Archiving and organisation: Creating structured digital archives that enable easy search and access. This can include categorising documents, tagging photos and videos with keywords and creating easily navigable folder structures.
- Data recovery and restoration: Help with the recovery of lost or damaged data from hard drives, USB sticks and other storage media.
- Advice on data security and data protection: Support in the implementation of security measures to ensure the privacy and security of digitised data.
- Training and support: Guidance for customers on how to effectively manage, access and secure their digitised data.

To successfully offer services in the field of digitalisation and organisation, you should consider the following steps:

- Market research: Understand the needs of your target group. Organisations may need help with compliance, while individuals may want to secure their personal memories.

- Investing in the right equipment: High-quality scanners and document management software are essential for providing efficient and high-quality services.
- Development of data protection guidelines: Data protection is particularly important if you work with sensitive information of your customers. Make sure you have clear guidelines and communicate them.
- Marketing and network building: Use online marketing, social media and networking events to promote your services. Word of mouth can also be a valuable source of new business.
- Ongoing training: Technology is constantly evolving. Keep up to date with new tools and best practices in the areas of digitalisation, data security and data protection.

The advantages for your customers are

- Improved access and search function: Digital documents are easier to find, access and share than physical documents.
- Space saving: Digitisation reduces the need for physical storage space.
- Increased security: Digital documents can be encrypted and backed up to prevent loss.
- Long-term preservation: Digital formats offer better opportunities for the long-term preservation of documents and media, free from physical deterioration.

By helping companies and individuals to digitise and organise their valuable data, you play an important role in making them future-proof and increasing their efficiency. With the right approach and the right tools, you can be a

E-sports training and coaching

If you are particularly skilled in certain video games, you offer coaching services for amateurs or semi-professional players who want to improve their skills.

Offering video game coaching services is an exciting and potentially lucrative business idea that capitalises on the growing world of e-sports and online gaming. With millions of gamers worldwide eager to improve their skills in various games, a niche is opening up for savvy gamers to share their knowledge and experience. Here are some steps and tips on how you can succeed as a gaming coach:

- Choose your games well: Focus on games in which you not only have extensive experience, but also in-depth knowledge of the strategies, mechanics and metagame. Popular games for coaching often include competitive titles such as "League of Legends", "Fortnite", "Counter-Strike: Global Offensive", "Dota 2" and many others.
- Stay up to date: In many games, the metagame changes regularly with updates or new content. To coach effectively, you always need to be up to date.

How to design your offer:

- Individualised coaching: Offer customised coaching sessions tailored to the specific needs and goals of each player. Some players may want to improve their general game strategies, while others may want to

work on specific aspects such as aim training in shooters or farming strategies in MOBAs.
- Group workshops: In addition to individual coaching sessions, you can also offer workshops for small groups to teach common skills and tactics.
- Video analysis: Offer to analyse gameplay footage to highlight strengths and weaknesses. This can be an effective method for providing concrete suggestions for improvement.

Marketing and customer acquisition:

- Build an online presence: Create a professional website or blog where you showcase your services, successes and reviews from past clients. Also use social media and gaming platforms to increase your visibility.
- Use gaming communities: Get involved in online forums and community sites that focus on your specialised games. This can help to demonstrate your expertise and attract potential customers.
- Streaming: Many successful coaches are also active streamers on platforms like Twitch or YouTube. Streaming can help you build a following, demonstrate your skills and interact directly with the community.
- Flexible pricing: Offer different packages, from individual sessions to more comprehensive coaching programmes. Take into account your experience, the value you offer and your competitors' prices.
- Additional resources: In addition to direct coaching sessions, consider offering supplementary resources such as guides, strategy documents or practice plans.

Always maintain a professional demeanour, both in your coaching sessions and in your online presence. Reliability, punctuality and respectful behaviour are essential.

Encourage fair playing practices and sportsmanship. As a coach, you have a role model function and should exemplify ethical behaviour both in and out of the game.

By combining your gaming skills with effective coaching and marketing, you can build a successful career in gaming coaching. Not only does it offer the opportunity to share your passion for video games, but also to help others achieve their goals.

Web development and design

Offering web design and development services for companies or individuals opens up a wide field with enormous opportunities. Creating a customised website, ranging from simple landing pages to complex e-commerce platforms, requires a deep understanding of both aesthetic design and technical functionality. In today's digital world, where a company's first impression is often made online, the demand for appealing and functional websites is greater than ever.

For web designers and developers, this means that they not only need to have a strong knowledge of design principles and user experience, but also technical skills in front-end and back-end development. The ability to design a website that works equally well on different devices while meeting the requirements of search engine optimisation is essential today.

The process of website design and development involves carefully planning and analysing the client's needs and goals in order to offer a customised solution that is precisely tailored to them. It's not just about the technical implementation, but also about telling a story and presenting a brand that stands out from the competition. The challenge is to find creative and innovative solutions that are both aesthetically pleasing and technically up to date.

Successful web design and development work also requires excellent project management skills and the ability to communicate effectively with clients. From the initial needs analysis, through project planning and the actual design and development phase, to the testing and launch of the website, it is important to continually engage the client and ensure that the final product meets expectations. In addition, offering maintenance and support services after the launch is crucial to keep the website up to date and to be able to respond quickly to any problems.

To attract clients for your web design and development services, a strong online presence is essential. This includes not only having a professional website that serves as a portfolio, but also actively using social media and participating in industry events and local business groups. Satisfied customers can help to expand your own network through recommendations and acquire new projects.

Overall, the field of web design and development offers creative and tech-savvy professionals the opportunity to create customised solutions that help companies and individuals strengthen their online presence and achieve their business goals. With the right skills, an understanding of current trends and technologies, and a strong customer focus, you can build a successful career in this field.

IT support and maintenance

Providing remote or on-site support for IT systems, network management and technical troubleshooting can be a lucrative business opportunity, especially for many small and medium-sized companies that often do not have their own IT department. This service is particularly valuable as the dependence on reliable IT systems is greater than ever in today's business world. Such a service can help companies increase their efficiency, minimise downtime and ultimately reduce their operating costs.

A key aspect of this business model is that it requires relatively little capital to get started compared to other ventures. The main investments are essentially limited to reliable hardware and software for your own use, a stable internet connection and possibly vehicle costs if the service includes on-site support. As many problems can be solved remotely, the technology opens up the possibility of serving customers not only locally, but also across greater geographical distances.

The service can cover a wide range of tasks, including setting up and maintaining computer networks, assisting with software and hardware issues, implementing cyber security measures and advising on the selection and deployment of new technologies. The ability to provide customised solutions tailored to each client's specific needs can add significant value and foster long-term client relationships.

To be successful, it is important not only to have extensive technical knowledge, but also to have excellent communication skills. The ability to explain complex technical concepts in layman's terms is crucial to building trust and understanding with your customers. In addition, building such a business requires a certain degree of flexibility and problem-solving skills, as you will be faced with a variety of technologies and challenges.

Marketing your services can be done through word of mouth, local advertising, a professional website and social media presence. A strong online presence can not only show potential clients your expertise and past successes, but also allow them to get in touch with you. Networking events and partnerships with other businesses can also be effective ways to attract new customers and publicise your service.

Overall, offering IT support services provides an excellent opportunity to address the technology challenges of small and medium-sized businesses while building a sustainable business. With the right knowledge, a customer-centric approach and effective marketing strategies, you can become a key resource for organisations looking to improve and secure their technology infrastructure.

Podcast editing

Provide editing services for podcasts, including audio editing, music, sound effects and improving overall audio quality.

Offering editing services for podcasts, ranging from audio editing to integrating music and sound effects to improving overall audio quality, is a specialised service that is in high demand in the growing podcast industry. With the increasing number of podcasts and the need for professional production to stand out from the crowd, your audio editing skills can help podcast creators take their content to the next level.

The process typically begins with the raw material recorded by the podcast creators. Their job is then to transform this material into a polished final product through careful cutting, arranging and editing. This can include removing unwanted sounds such as pauses, ums and background noise to create a clearer and more professional listening experience. In addition, adding music and sound effects can help create the desired atmosphere and increase listener attention.

An important aspect of your service is also improving the overall audio quality. This can include adjusting levels, balancing audio tracks and applying effects such as equalisation (EQ), compression and reverb to ensure a consistent and enjoyable listening experience throughout the episode. The ability to work with different audio formats and software, as well as a good ear for detail, are crucial for success in this field.

To market your services, it's important to have a strong online presence that showcases your past work and experience. A professional website, active social media profiles and examples of your work can attract potential clients. Networking in podcast communities, attending industry events and offering sample edits can also be effective ways to attract new clients and build confidence in your abilities.

Editing podcasts requires not only technical skills, but also creativity and a good understanding of storytelling and timing. Working with podcast creators to understand their vision and goals is an essential part of the process. By offering customised editing services tailored to the needs of each individual podcast, you can make a valuable contribution to the production of high quality and engaging podcasts that delight both creators and listeners.

Development of mobile apps

If you have knowledge of mobile app development, you can develop customised solutions for companies or your own apps that target specific needs or interests. With platforms such as Google Play or the Apple App Store, you can make your apps accessible to a wide audience.

Developing customised solutions for businesses or creating your own apps that target specific needs or interests is a great way to use your expertise in mobile app development. In a world where smartphones and tablets have become indispensable parts of everyday life, the demand for customised mobile applications is constantly increasing. These applications can range from simple productivity tools to complex systems that optimise business processes or offer entirely new user experiences.

By publishing your apps on platforms such as Google Play or the Apple App Store, you can make your creations accessible to a global audience. This not only opens the door to a huge market, but also offers the opportunity to generate revenue through direct sales, subscriptions, in-app purchases or advertising. The key to success lies in developing applications that are not only innovative and user-friendly, but also offer real added value for your target audience.

To be successful in this dynamic environment, it is crucial to follow current trends in mobile app development and to develop a deep understanding of the needs and wishes of your target group. This requires continuous training and adaptation to new technologies and platforms. In addition, it is important to have a good sense of design and user experience in order to develop apps that are not only functional, but also visually appealing and intuitive to use.

Successfully marketing your apps requires a clear strategy, which can range from search engine optimisation (SEO) for app stores to social media marketing and partnerships with influencers. A strong online presence that highlights your apps and their benefits is just as important as collecting and utilising user feedback to continuously improve and update your products.

By developing customised solutions for companies or creating your own apps that focus on specific needs or interests, you can not only use your technical skills and creativity, but also tap into revenue streams. With dedication, an innovative spirit and an understanding of your target audience's needs, you can succeed in the world of mobile app development and make a lasting impact.

Cybersecurity consulting

In today's digitally connected world, the threat of cyberattacks is a constant and growing challenge for organisations of all sizes. With the increasing complexity and sophistication of cyber threats, more and more organisations are recognising the need to protect their digital assets. This creates a significant demand for cybersecurity professionals who can help organisations strengthen their security strategies. If you have experience and knowledge in cybersecurity, security consulting offers an excellent opportunity to utilise your skills and help companies arm themselves against potential threats.

Your services could cover a wide range of activities, from conducting security audits, where you evaluate an organisation's existing security systems, to risk assessment, where you identify and evaluate potential vulnerabilities, to the development and implementation of comprehensive security measures. These measures could include technical solutions as well as guidelines and training for employees to promote comprehensive security awareness.

Success in this field requires not only a deep technical understanding of the various aspects of cybersecurity, such as network security, application security and data encryption, but also the ability to communicate complex security concepts clearly and develop customised solutions that meet the specific requirements of each company. In addition, it is important to continuously educate yourself and stay up to date, as both technology and the nature of threats are constantly evolving.

Marketing your services requires a clear strategy that highlights your expertise and track record in cybersecurity. Building a strong online presence, attending industry conferences and networking with other professionals can be effective ways to reach potential clients. Satisfied customers can also be a valuable source of referrals and repeat business.

By offering your services as a cybersecurity consultant, you can play a crucial role in protecting organisations from the potentially devastating effects of cyberattacks. With the right approach and commitment, you can not only contribute to the security of digital infrastructures, but also build a successful and fulfilling business.

Cloud computing services

Offering consultancy and management services to organisations looking to move their infrastructure to the cloud is meeting a growing demand in the modern business world.

Migrating to the cloud offers numerous benefits, including cost efficiency, scalability, flexibility and improved collaboration. However, the transition can be complex and challenging, prompting many organisations to look for experts who can guide them through the process.

As a consultant in this area, you would help organisations select the most suitable cloud platform for their specific needs, be it Amazon Web Services (AWS), Microsoft Azure, Google Cloud Platform (GCP) or another. This requires a deep understanding of the various cloud services and models, as well as industry-specific requirements and compliance standards.

Migrating data and applications to the cloud is a critical step that needs to be carefully planned and executed to avoid data loss or business disruption. They would help organisations develop a customised migration strategy that includes the transfer of data, applications and workloads while ensuring the integrity and security of the data.

Following successful migration to the cloud, ongoing management of cloud resources is critical to optimising performance, security and cost efficiency. This can include monitoring systems, managing access rights, implementing security measures and regularly assessing the cloud architecture to ensure it meets changing business requirements.

To be successful in this field, it is important to have extensive knowledge of cloud computing, network architecture, database management and cyber security. In addition, strong analytical skills and the ability to communicate complex technical concepts clearly and comprehensibly are crucial.

Marketing your services can be done by building a strong online presence, attending industry conferences, writing professional articles and networking with other IT professionals.

Recommendations from satisfied customers and case studies highlighting successful migration projects can also be valuable tools to build trust with potential customers and grow your business.

By providing cloud migration consulting and management services, you can play a key role in helping organisations to harness the benefits of cloud technology while minimising challenges and risks. With the right expertise and approach, you have the opportunity to make a significant impact on the success and efficiency of organisations in the digital era.

Data analysis and reporting

Using your data analytics skills to help organisations gain valuable insights from their data represents a significant business opportunity in today's data-driven economy. Companies of all sizes are generating an ever-growing amount of data that can potentially provide valuable insights into customer behaviour, market trends, operational efficiency and much more. The key is to effectively collect, analyse and interpret this data to make informed strategic decisions.

Your role as a data analyst would involve sifting through complex data sets and extracting understandable, actionable insights to help organisations improve performance, minimise risks and identify new opportunities. This could include creating detailed reports and dashboards, visualising data for easier interpretation and recommending actions based on your analysis.

To be successful in this role, it is critical to have advanced knowledge of data analytics, experience with analytics tools and software such as SQL, Python, R, as well as BI tools such as Tableau or Power BI. Equally important is an understanding of business processes and the ability to communicate complex analyses and concepts clearly and effectively to ensure that your recommendations can be understood and implemented.

The challenge is not only to analyse data, but also to present the results in a context that is relevant to the business. This requires close collaboration with stakeholders to understand their needs and objectives and ensure that your analyses address them. In addition, regular reviews of the measures implemented and their impact on business performance can help to emphasise the value of your services and promote long-term partnerships.

Marketing your services could be done by building a strong online presence, sharing case studies and success stories on your website and social media, as well as networking at industry-related events. Recommendations and testimonials from satisfied customers can also be a powerful tool to build credibility and open up new business opportunities.

By helping organisations gain valuable insights from their data, you play a critical role in enabling them to make informed decisions that lead to growth and success. With the right skills and a strategic approach, you can become a sought-after resource in the landscape of the modern business world.

Software development

Developing customised software solutions for specific industry needs or common problems presents a unique opportunity to drive profound change in the way businesses and individuals achieve their goals. By offering customised software solutions, you can directly address the individual needs and challenges of your customers, whether by optimising business processes, enhancing learning experiences or enriching entertainment opportunities. The range of applications is almost limitless, from business applications that increase operational efficiency, to educational software that personalises learning, to entertainment apps that enable new forms of interaction and enjoyment.

The key to success in this area lies in the ability to not only provide technical expertise in software development, but also to have a deep understanding of the specific challenges and opportunities within the respective industries. This requires working closely with customers to fully understand their requirements and develop solutions that not only meet but exceed those requirements.

Developing customised software solutions requires a wide range of technical skills, including programming, database management, user interface design and system integration. In addition, project management skills are critical to ensure that projects are completed on time, within budget and to the client's specifications.

Another challenge is to constantly educate yourself and keep up with the latest technological developments. The technology landscape is changing rapidly and to stay competitive, you need to be able to integrate the latest tools, frameworks and best practices into your work.

Marketing your bespoke software development services can be done by building a strong online presence, showcasing your projects and successes on your website and social media, and networking in relevant industry circles. Case studies and testimonials from satisfied clients can give potential customers confidence that you have the skills and experience required to overcome their specific challenges.

By developing customised software solutions that are specifically tailored to your customers' needs, you can not only solve significant business and personal challenges, but also build lasting relationships with your customers and make a valuable contribution to their success. With the right combination of technical expertise, industry knowledge and a customer-centric approach, you have the opportunity to succeed in this dynamic and ever-evolving field.

Blockchain development

The growing interest in blockchain technologies provides a unique opportunity for professionals with knowledge in this area to offer innovative services. Blockchain, the technology behind cryptocurrencies such as Bitcoin and Ethereum, has the potential to transform industries far beyond the financial sector. From improving security and transparency in supply chains to creating new forms of digital identity, the potential applications are diverse and revolutionary.

By offering services in the development of smart contracts, decentralised applications (DApps) or consulting on blockchain strategies, you position yourself at the forefront of a technological wave that aims to redefine the way business and daily transactions are conducted. Smart contracts, self-executing contracts with the terms of the agreement written directly into code, provide a secure and automated way to execute agreements without the need for a central authority. Decentralised applications (DApps) run on a blockchain network and benefit from its advantages such as immutability, transparency and resistance to censorship.

Providing these services requires a deep technical understanding of blockchain technology, including knowledge of relevant programming languages such as Solidity for Ethereum-based applications, as well as a comprehensive understanding of the specific challenges and opportunities that blockchain offers. In addition, it is important to understand the business and legal aspects of blockchain projects to ensure that the solutions developed are not only technically sound, but also practically feasible and compliant with existing laws and regulations.

To be successful, you must not only have technical skills, but also be able to communicate complex concepts clearly and help clients understand the strategic benefits of blockchain technology for their business. This requires a strong ability to problem solve and innovate, as well as a willingness to continuously learn and adapt as blockchain technology and the regulatory environment evolve.

Marketing your blockchain services can be done by attending industry conferences, publishing articles and studies on blockchain topics, and actively engaging in blockchain communities and social media. Building a strong brand as a blockchain expert can help build trust with potential customers and differentiate your services from the competition.

By offering services in the area of smart contract development, DApps or blockchain strategy consulting, you can help companies and organisations take advantage of this disruptive technology while making a valuable contribution to shaping the future of digital transactions and interactions. With the right combination of technical expertise, strategic thinking and a deep understanding of the potential applications and impact of blockchain technology, you can succeed in this exciting and rapidly evolving field.

Digital marketing and SEO

Offering digital marketing services aimed at improving the online presence and visibility of companies is essential in today's increasingly digitalised world. Digitalisation has fundamentally changed the way companies communicate and interact with their target groups. A strong online presence is no longer just an advantage, but a necessity for a company's success and growth. By offering a comprehensive range of digital marketing services, such as search engine optimisation (SEO), content marketing, social media management and email marketing, you can help companies increase their brand awareness, interact with their target audience and ultimately increase their sales.

Search engine optimisation (SEO) plays a crucial role in improving a website's visibility in search engine results, leading directly to increased traffic and potential customers. SEO encompasses a range of techniques and strategies, including optimising web content and meta tags as well as improving website structure and performance to improve rankings in search results.

Content marketing focuses on the creation and distribution of valuable, relevant and consistent content to attract and retain a defined target audience. Through informative and engaging content, companies can build authority and trust in their industry, which ultimately leads to increased customer retention and conversion.

Social media management is crucial for promoting brand awareness and building relationships with customers. By strategically utilising social media platforms, you can help companies effectively spread their message, receive direct feedback from customers and build a community of loyal followers.

Email marketing provides a direct line of communication to customers and potential customers and remains one of the most cost-effective methods of increasing engagement, brand awareness and sales. By developing targeted email campaigns, you can send personalised messages that are tailored to the specific needs and interests of recipients.

To be successful in providing digital marketing services, it is important to not only have expertise in the various disciplines of digital marketing, but also a deep understanding of your clients' goals and challenges. This requires continuous training and adaptation to the ever-changing trends and technologies in the digital marketing landscape.

Marketing your services can be done by building a strong online presence of your own, participating in networking events, creating thought leadership content and collecting client reviews. By delivering demonstrable results and measurable ROI for your clients, you can build long-term relationships and successfully grow your digital marketing business.

Artificial intelligence (AI) and machine learning

Having expertise in artificial intelligence (AI) and machine learning (ML) opens up a wide range of opportunities to develop innovative solutions or offer consulting services that help companies automate and optimise their processes. In an era where data is being generated in unprecedented volume and velocity, AI and ML can be critical tools to extract valuable insights from this data, improve decision-making processes and increase operational efficiency.

AI and ML technologies have the potential to transform almost every aspect of business, from customer interaction and marketing to product development and supply chain management. By developing customised AI solutions or offering consulting services, you can help companies identify patterns and trends in data that human analysts might miss. These technologies also make it possible to perform predictive analyses that can help companies predict future trends and plan accordingly.

The development of AI-driven applications can range from automating routine tasks, to improving customer service through chatbots and virtual assistants, to optimising logistics and inventory management. In addition, AI and ML can be used in product development to design new products and services that are better tailored to the needs and wishes of customers.

AI and ML consulting services can help organisations identify the technologies best suited to their specific needs, develop implementation strategies and create the necessary data architectures. An important aspect of consulting is also to help organisations navigate the ethical and legal considerations associated with the use of AI to ensure that they act responsibly and in accordance with applicable regulations.

To be successful, it is crucial to have not only technical skills in AI and ML, but also a deep understanding of business processes and challenges in different industries. This requires strong analytical skills, creativity in problem solving and the ability to communicate complex technical concepts in a way that non-experts can understand.

Marketing your AI and ML services can be done by building a strong online presence, presenting case studies and success stories and actively networking in relevant industries. By offering workshops, presentations and publications, you can also establish yourself as a thought leader in the field and build trust with potential clients.

By developing innovative solutions or providing consulting services in AI and ML, you can help organisations gain a competitive advantage, increase efficiency and unlock new growth opportunities. With the right combination of technical expertise, business understanding and strategic thinking, you can contribute to your clients' success while building a successful business in the field of artificial intelligence and machine learning.

Freelance data analysis

The idea of starting your own business as a freelance data analyst is particularly attractive for start-ups without significant start-up capital. Data analysis is an area that is becoming increasingly important in the modern business world. Companies of all sizes and industries collect large amounts of data, from customer information to performance indicators. However, the mere existence of this data does not guarantee business success. The key lies in analysing and interpreting this data in order to derive strategic decisions. This is exactly where the freelance data analyst comes in.

The first step on this path is to ensure that you have the necessary skills and knowledge in data analysis. This includes not only mastering analytical tools and techniques, but also a deep understanding of statistical methods and the ability to interpret complex data sets. It is also important to keep learning and staying up to date, as tools and methods in this field are evolving rapidly.

As the initial investment is comparatively low - you essentially only need a powerful computer and possibly a few software licences - freelance data analysis is ideal for start-ups without large amounts of capital. The focus is more on the acquisition of knowledge and skills than on financial investment.

Building up a customer base is one of the biggest challenges at the beginning. Networking is essential here. Utilise professional networks such as LinkedIn, attend industry events and possibly offer your services at a discounted rate initially to gather references and demonstrate your results. A good strategy is also to specialise in a niche or industry in which you already have experience or a particular interest. This will allow you to position yourself as an expert in this field and make it easier to approach potential customers.

Another important aspect is the presentation of your work results. The ability to translate complex analyses into understandable reports or presentations that directly support business decisions is critical to your success. Your customers are looking for valuable insights that they can implement directly, not complicated statistical analyses that they don't understand.

In practice, this could mean analysing customer purchase patterns for an online retailer to optimise stock levels, or evaluating the effectiveness of marketing campaigns for a small business to improve ROI. The possibilities are diverse and span almost all industries.

In conclusion, self-employment in the field of data analytics is a rewarding and accessible option for start-ups without large start-up capital. The challenges lie less in the financial aspect and more in the need to continually learn, build a network and market your skills effectively. However, with dedication and the right skills, you can build a successful career as a freelance data analyst.

Counselling and coaching

Personal training and coaching

The idea of offering personal training and coaching services is an excellent business opportunity for those with certification and in-depth knowledge of fitness and nutrition. This area has grown significantly in popularity in recent years, not least because of a growing awareness of health and well-being among the population. In addition, the pandemic has accelerated the acceptance and demand for virtual training and coaching services, opening up new opportunities for those willing to offer their services both in person and online.

The first step for aspiring personal trainers and coaches is often to obtain a recognised certification. Such certifications not only confirm your competence and credibility in the eyes of potential clients, but also provide valuable knowledge about training principles, nutritional counselling and client care. In addition, it is important to continually educate yourself to stay on top of the latest science and practice in fitness, nutrition and health coaching.

The initial investment for such an endeavour can be relatively low, especially if you initially focus on online coaching. To run virtual training sessions, you will need a good internet connection, a suitable device (laptop, tablet or smartphone) and possibly additional software or apps for training and client management. If you want to offer face-to-face training, the costs could be higher, depending on whether you need to invest in equipment or rent premises.

To be successful, it is essential to build a strong online presence and develop effective marketing strategies. A professionally designed website, active social media profiles and positive customer reviews can go a long way in building trust with potential clients and promoting your services. In addition, offering free trials or informational materials about fitness and health can help generate interest and build a relationship with potential clients.

The flexibility to offer both in-person and virtual services opens up a wide range of possibilities. In-person training offers the benefit of direct interaction and the ability to make specific techniques and corrections, which can be especially valuable for clients with specific needs or pre-existing conditions. Virtual coaching, on the other hand, offers flexibility and accessibility for clients who are remote or have busy schedules.

A successful personal training and coaching business requires not only expertise in fitness and nutrition, but also strong interpersonal skills. The ability to be motivational, empathetic and personalised to each client's needs and goals is crucial to building long-term client relationships. By combining expertise, effective marketing and excellent customer service, you can build a loyal client base and establish yourself as a trusted and competent provider in this growing market.

Online event planning

The planning and coordination of online events is an area that has grown enormously in importance in recent years. The digital transformation and the circumstances of recent global events have prompted companies, organisations and individuals to increasingly switch to virtual events. From virtual conferences and seminars to online weddings and birthday parties in the digital space - the possibilities are many and varied and offer enormous potential for start-ups wishing to specialise in this sector.

No large investments are initially required to get started in online event planning, which makes this area particularly attractive for founders without extensive start-up capital. However, basic technical know-how, organisational skills and an understanding of the latest digital tools and platforms are essential. Knowledge in areas such as video conferencing technologies, virtual event platforms, social media and online marketing is a great advantage.

The challenge when planning online events is to create a unique and engaging experience that connects participants despite the physical distance. This includes not only the technical implementation, but also the creative design of the programme, the selection of suitable entertainment offerings and the promotion of interaction between the participants. To successfully establish yourself in this field, it is important to specialise in certain types of events and develop unique concepts that set your services apart from the competition.

Being a successful online event planner also means staying up to date and familiarising yourself with the latest trends and technologies. The digital world is evolving rapidly and what is innovative today may be outdated tomorrow. Continuous training and a willingness to learn new tools and methods are therefore essential.

A strong online presence is crucial to attracting customers. A professional website that clearly presents your offering and showcases examples of successful events, as well as active social media channels, are important tools for reaching your target audience and building trust. Networking, both online and in person, can also help to promote your business. Referrals from satisfied customers are often the key to success in the events industry.

Ultimately, planning and organising online events requires a high degree of flexibility, creativity and technical understanding. The ability to cater to the individual needs and wishes of your customers and make each event a unique and memorable experience will help you to position yourself successfully in this growing market. With commitment and the right strategy, online event planning offers exciting opportunities for entrepreneurs who are ready to break new ground.

Consultancy for remote work and virtual teams

Remote working and virtual team consulting represents a timely and increasingly relevant business idea, especially in light of the global shift towards more flexible working models. This change has been accelerated by technological advances as well as external factors such as the global pandemic, which has caused organisations of all sizes and industries to re-evaluate the way they work. However, the shift to remote working is a challenge for many organisations, providing an excellent opportunity for start-ups looking to specialise in consultancy in this area.

As a remote work and virtual team consultant, you would help organisations create efficient and effective virtual working environments. This includes a variety of services, from technical setup and selection of appropriate tools to developing strategies for communication, collaboration and company culture. A key aspect of your work would be advising on best practices for remote management, including leading virtual teams, maintaining employee motivation and retention, and fostering a strong corporate culture in a distributed work environment.

To be successful in this area, it is important not only to have a sound knowledge of the technologies and platforms available for remote working, but also to have a deep understanding of the human aspects of remote working. This includes knowledge of the challenges faced by individuals and teams, as well as strategies to overcome these challenges. Your ability to develop customised solutions that address both the technical and social needs of your clients will be a key to your success.

The demand for consultancy services in this area offers the opportunity to serve a wide range of clients - from small and medium-sized businesses to large corporations looking to optimise their existing remote working policies. You could also offer workshops, training and webinars to equip individuals and teams with the necessary skills and knowledge to work successfully in a virtual environment.

The marketing strategy for your consultancy should aim to highlight your expertise and successes in helping businesses make the transition to remote working. A strong online presence, including a professional website and active social media channels, is crucial to reaching your target audience. Content marketing, such as publishing articles, blog posts and case studies, can also help to demonstrate your expertise and attract potential clients.

In summary, remote work and virtual team consulting offers a promising business opportunity for start-ups that have the necessary technical and soft skills. By helping organisations overcome the challenges of remote working and build efficient, productive and happy virtual teams, you can make a valuable contribution to your clients' success while building a successful career in a cutting-edge field.

Self-defence courses

The provision of self-defence courses, whether online or face-to-face, addresses a fundamental human need: the feeling of safety. In a world where concern for personal safety is on the rise, self-defence courses offer a valuable skill that can boost participants' confidence and provide them with practical techniques to defend themselves in potentially dangerous situations. This area therefore offers an excellent business opportunity for start-ups who have the necessary skills and knowledge in self-defence techniques.

One of the keys to success in this business is to develop a comprehensive and accessible training programme aimed at people of different ages and physical conditions. This could include offering different courses tailored to specific needs, such as courses for women, children, seniors or even specialised workshops for companies and organisations. The ability to create bespoke programmes that cater to the individual needs and abilities of participants will not only improve the effectiveness of training, but also help to reach a wider audience.

For face-to-face classes, it is important to find suitable facilities that are safe and accessible. These could be rented in gyms, community centres or schools, depending on availability and budget. The advantage of face-to-face interaction is that techniques can be demonstrated and corrected directly, which is often essential for learning physical self-defence skills.

Online courses, on the other hand, open up the possibility of reaching an even wider audience, including people who are unable to attend in person due to geographical or time constraints. To run online courses, you will need a stable internet connection, high-quality camera equipment and possibly a platform for course management and delivery. The challenge with online courses is to maintain the engagement and interaction of the participants and to ensure that the techniques taught are carried out correctly.

Regardless of whether you choose online or face-to-face courses, marketing is an essential aspect of your business. A strong online presence through a professional website, active social media channels and positive customer reviews can be crucial to building credibility and attracting new customers. In addition, offering free introductory workshops or demonstration courses can be an effective strategy to generate interest and demonstrate the value of your courses.

Success in delivering self-defence courses depends not only on your skills as a trainer, but also on your ability to create a supportive and empowering environment. Participants should feel safe to learn and practice new skills, and they should be encouraged to develop their confidence and skills. By combining high quality training with a strong focus on customer satisfaction and safety, you can build a successful business that has a positive and lasting impact on the lives of your customers.

Consultancy for sustainability

Sustainability consulting is an increasingly sought-after service as both businesses and individuals strive to minimise their environmental impact and adopt more sustainable practices. This trend is driven by growing awareness of environmental issues, consumer pressure on companies to act more responsibly and regulatory requirements. As a start-up in the field of sustainability consulting, there are many opportunities for you to make a positive impact on the environment while building a successful business.

Firstly, it is important that you have a sound knowledge of environmental protection, sustainable development and green technologies. Training or certification in a relevant field can increase your credibility and expertise in the eyes of potential clients. In addition, it is crucial to continuously educate yourself and stay up to date, as sustainability best practices and available technologies are constantly evolving.

As a sustainability consultant, you can offer a wide range of services aimed at reducing your clients' environmental footprint. These include, for example:

- Waste management and reduction: Help businesses and individuals minimise their waste production,

- implement effective recycling programmes and develop zero-waste strategies.
- Energy efficiency: Advise customers on the selection and implementation of energy-efficient solutions, from the insulation of their buildings to the use of LED lighting and energy-efficient appliances.
- Renewable energies: Help businesses and households switch to renewable energy sources, whether by installing solar panels or utilising wind energy.
- Sustainable procurement: Advise companies on the selection of sustainable materials and products and support them in establishing responsible supply chains.
- Carbon footprint and climate neutrality: Help customers calculate their carbon footprint and develop strategies to reduce and offset their greenhouse gas emissions.

To be successful, it is important that you not only have technical expertise, but also strong communication skills to convey complex concepts clearly and convince customers of the benefits of sustainable practices. A customised approach that takes into account the specific needs and goals of each client is often the most effective.

Building a network and presence in relevant forums and at events can also help to publicise your consultancy. A strong online presence, including a professional website and active social media profiles, is essential to reach your target audience and showcase your expertise.

Sustainability consulting offers not only the opportunity to run a successful business, but also to make a significant contribution to protecting the environment and promoting a more sustainable future. By combining expertise, a passion for environmental issues and a client-centred approach, you can help businesses and individuals make positive changes that deliver both economic and environmental benefits.

E-learning platforms and content

The development of e-learning platforms and content is a promising business idea, especially at a time when digital education and distance learning are becoming increasingly important. This industry offers a wide range of opportunities, from providing specialised courses in technical skills to programmes that teach soft skills. For founders without significant start-up capital, this sector is particularly attractive as the creation of digital education content often involves relatively little initial investment, provided you have the necessary knowledge and skills.

One of the first steps in building a business in e-learning is to identify a niche or a need that is not yet adequately met. Although the market for online education can be competitive, there are significant opportunities to be had by specialising in certain subject areas or target groups. For example, this could be a course for a specific programming language, a programme to improve emotional intelligence in the workplace or courses aimed at specific professional groups.

Once you have decided on a topic or area, the next step is to develop high-quality, engaging content. In digital education, the quality of the content and the way it is presented is critical to success. Various formats can be used, including video tutorials, interactive tasks, text lessons and discussion forums. The variety of formats helps to cater for different learning styles and increase learner engagement.

Technically, developing e-learning content requires knowledge of content creation and possibly the use of specific software to create learning materials and platforms. Open source learning management systems such as Moodle offer a cost-effective way to host and manage your courses, while tools such as Articulate Storyline or Adobe Captivate can be used to create interactive learning content. For those with limited technical skills, platforms such as Teachable or Udemy offer a user-friendly environment to create and deliver courses without having to invest in in-house website development.

Marketing your courses and platforms is crucial to reach your target audience and generate enrolments. Strategies can include social media marketing, content marketing (e.g. blogging, webinars), search engine optimisation (SEO) and partnerships with other education providers or companies. Offering free trial content or mini-courses can also be an effective way to attract potential customers and give them a taste of what you offer.

Creating a successful e-learning business requires a passion for education, a commitment to quality and a willingness to continually adapt to the changing needs of learners. Despite the challenges and competition, the digital education market offers significant growth opportunities and the chance to make a positive impact on the lives of people worldwide. With the right idea, a well thought-out strategy and a focus on quality, even founders without substantial start-up capital can succeed in this exciting and fulfilling field.

Craft and production

Sustainable fashion

Creating and selling sustainable or upcycled fashion items online is not only a business idea with enormous growth potential, but also appeals to an increasingly environmentally conscious audience that values sustainability, ethics and uniqueness in fashion. This business idea is particularly suitable for founders without large start-up capital, as it can be realised with relatively low initial investment and offers plenty of scope for creativity.

Steps to starting a sustainable fashion business

- Find your niche: Sustainable fashion is a broad field. Focus on a niche that matches your passion, be it upcycled clothing, handmade accessories or fashion made from recycled materials. Specialising will help you stand out from the competition and appeal to a specific target group.
- Sourcing of materials: For a sustainable fashion company, the procurement of materials is of crucial importance. Look for suppliers of recycled or sustainably sourced fabrics and materials. Flea markets, second-hand shops and fabric remnants from other designers can also be excellent sources of upcycled materials.
- Design and production: Develop a collection that reflects your brand and values. Start with a small but select range of items to keep initial costs low and get feedback from your first customers. If you can't or

- don't want to produce yourself, look for local manufacturers or artisans who share your vision and support ethical labour practices.
- Online presence and sales: A strong online presence is crucial to building your brand and selling your products. Create an engaging online shop with platforms like Shopify, Etsy or Big Cartel that are user-friendly and offer e-commerce features. Use social media to promote your products, tell your story and build a community around your brand.
- Marketing and storytelling: Sustainable fashion is not just about products, but also about the stories behind the items. Use your marketing to emphasise the origin of your materials, the production process and the people behind the scenes. Authenticity and transparency are key to building trust and loyalty with your target group.
- Focus on sustainability: Be consistent in your commitment to sustainability in all aspects of your business, from packaging to shipping. Customers who value sustainable fashion pay attention to these details.

Advantages and challenges

Offering sustainable fashion items not only offers the opportunity to build a profitable business, but also to make a positive contribution to reducing fashion waste and promoting environmentally friendly practices. However, one challenge could be convincing consumers to accept a potentially higher price for sustainable products. The key here is to emphasise the value and longevity of the products as well as the positive environmental impact.

Overall, starting a sustainable fashion business offers an exciting opportunity to combine creativity and entrepreneurial spirit to make a real difference in the world. With passion, hard work and a clear focus on sustainability, you can build a loyal customer base and contribute to change in the fashion industry.

Environmentally friendly and sustainable business models

Virtual tour guides

The concept of virtual tour guides offers an innovative business idea that represents a great opportunity in today's increasingly digitalised world. With the advent of virtual reality (VR) and other technologies, it has become possible to create immersive travel experiences without tourists having to leave their homes. This is particularly attractive for people who are unable or unwilling to travel for various reasons, whether due to lack of time, financial constraints or health concerns. In addition, the global pandemic has increased interest and demand for virtual travel experiences.

The development of virtual tours focussing on specific areas of interest such as history, art or architecture requires thorough research and planning. Topics should be selected based on market research and potential interest. It is important to create unique and engaging content that offers users not only informative but also emotionally appealing experiences.

From a technical point of view, virtual tours can be created using various software tools and platforms designed for the development of VR and 360-degree video content. Knowledge of video editing, VR technology and digital content creation is an advantage. In addition, partnerships with museums, historical sites and cultural institutions can improve the authenticity and depth of the tours offered.

Another aspect that should be considered when designing virtual travel experiences is accessibility. Tours should be designed to work flawlessly on different devices, from PCs and tablets to smartphones and VR headsets. This ensures that a wide audience is reached and that the user experience is optimised.

To market the virtual tours, an effective online presence is crucial. A professionally designed website that provides detailed information about the tours on offer, previews and customer reviews can attract potential customers. Social media channels and online marketing campaigns can also be utilised to create awareness and generate interest. In addition, collaborations with travel blogs, educational institutions and cultural organisations can provide further channels to promote the virtual tours.

Offering virtual tour guides is not only a business opportunity, but also a chance to share culture, history and knowledge in innovative ways and connect people worldwide. By combining technological expertise, creative content creation and effective marketing, you can build a successful virtual travel experience business and reach a wide audience.

Travel planning, online travel agency

The idea of setting up an online travel agency or specialising in individual travel planning is an attractive option for start-ups without a lot of start-up capital. Although the travel market is highly competitive, it also offers numerous niches and opportunities to stand out with creative and personalised services. The key to success in this area is to create unique travel experiences that go beyond the offerings of traditional travel agencies.

Steps to setting up an online travel agency or specialising in travel planning:

- Identify a market niche: Focus on specific types of travel or target groups. This could be sustainable travel, adventure travel, luxury travel, specific regions or travel for certain demographics such as seniors, families or solo travellers. A well-defined niche will help you stand out from the competition and develop a targeted marketing strategy.
- Build relationships: Network with providers of accommodation, tours, transport and other travel services. Strong partnerships are key to providing your customers with attractive offers and unique experiences. This can also help you negotiate special conditions or discounts that make your offers more competitive.
- Establish an online presence: A professional website is essential to the success of your online travel agency. The website should be user-friendly, offer attractive photos and descriptions of the destinations and include the option to book or enquire about holidays directly. Social media channels can also be used to promote offers and interact with potential customers.
- Offer personalised services: The added value of your business can lie in personalisation. Offer customised itineraries, insider tips and personal

- recommendations tailored to the individual interests and needs of your customers. This can range from booking accommodation and flights to planning detailed itineraries and special experiences.
- Marketing and customer acquisition: Develop a marketing strategy to reach your target audience. This can include content marketing, search engine optimisation (SEO), paid online advertising and collecting customer reviews. Word of mouth and recommendations from satisfied customers can also be an effective way to attract new customers.
- Quality and customer service: Excellent customer service and the provision of high-quality holidays are crucial for long-term success. Quick and personalised responses to enquiries, support with problems during the trip and obtaining feedback after the trip can help to build a loyal customer base.

Entering the travel industry as an online travel agency or as a specialist in customised travel planning requires commitment and hard work, but offers the opportunity to turn a passion for travel into a successful business. With creative ideas, excellent customer service and a strong online presence, you can establish and grow in this exciting field.

Event and experience offers

For start-ups without large amounts of capital, there are numerous creative business ideas in the events and festivals sector that can be realised with a low initial investment and clever use of resources. Here are some ideas that are primarily based on services rather than physical products, which can keep the initial investment low:

Mobile catering and food trucks

Getting into the mobile catering and food truck business can be an excellent business idea for start-ups without a lot of start-up capital. The key is to specialise in a particular type of food or drink that is popular at events and festivals, and to manage resources skilfully. Here are some detailed steps and considerations that can help you get started:

- Market research: Start with thorough market research to find out what types of food or drink are particularly popular with your target group. Look at current trends, visit local events and festivals to see what is popular and where there may be a gap in the market.
- Specialisation: Decide on a specific offer that is not only popular but also practical to implement. For example, you could specialise in gourmet burgers, vegetarian or vegan dishes, special types of coffee or fresh smoothies. A clear specialisation helps you to stand out from other providers.
- Equipment and food truck: Initially, you can save costs by purchasing used equipment or a second-hand food truck. Make sure that all equipment meets local health standards. You could also consider a small stall or mobile vending cart before investing in a fully equipped food truck.
- Location and events: Choose your locations and events carefully. A good location can be crucial for

success. Start with smaller local events to publicise your brand and gain experience. Network with event organisers and secure places at larger festivals.
- Licences and permits: Find out about all the necessary licences and permits you need to operate a food truck. This can vary depending on the location and usually includes health checks, business registrations and special permits for selling on public land.
- Marketing: Develop a strong brand and use social media to reach your target audience. Attractive pictures of your dishes, participation in food truck rallies and special offers can help build a loyal customer base. Word of mouth is also very valuable, so strive for high quality and excellent customer service.
- Scaling: Once your business takes off, think about ways to scale. This could include expanding to multiple trucks, expanding the menu or even switching to catering for private functions or corporate events.

By focusing on these key areas, you can create a solid foundation for your mobile catering and food truck business and grow it successfully, even with limited initial capital.

Event planning and coordination

Offering services as an event planner can be a rewarding business idea for founders without significant start-up capital, as it mainly depends on expertise, organisational skills and networking abilities. Here are some detailed steps and considerations that can help you succeed as an event planner:

- Define your niche: Determine what kind of events you want to plan. This could focus on certain types of

private celebrations such as weddings, birthdays and anniversaries or on business events such as conferences, workshops and company parties. You could also specialise in cultural events, music festivals or sporting events. A clear niche choice will help you to carry out targeted marketing and position yourself as an expert.
- Build expertise: Although formal qualifications are not mandatory, training or certification in event management can boost your credibility. It's also important to stay on top of the latest industry trends and standards so you can offer your clients innovative and up-to-date solutions.
- Marketing and presence: Since your main investment is time and marketing, you should develop effective strategies to promote your services. Create a professional website and use social media to showcase your projects and share customer reviews. Networking events in your industry and collaborations with other service providers such as caterers, decorators and equipment hire companies can also be very valuable.
- Tools and resources: Use modern technologies and software solutions to optimise your work processes. This includes tools for project management, budgeting, scheduling and communication. Many of these tools are available at low cost or even free of charge and can help you work more efficiently and provide a professional service.
- Building and maintaining customer relationships: The satisfaction of your customers is crucial to the success of your business. Provide excellent customer service and make sure to exceed your customers' expectations. Word of mouth from satisfied customers

can be one of the most powerful tools for growing your business.
- Scaling your business: Once you have built up a stable customer base, you can consider how you can expand your business. You may hire additional staff, expand your range of services or specialise further in a particular event category.

By focussing on these key aspects, you can be successful as an event planner, even if you are starting out with limited financial resources. The key lies in the quality of your service, your commitment to your clients and your ability to respond effectively to their needs.

Leisure activities and workshops

Offering interactive activities such as art workshops, dance classes or yoga sessions at festivals is a great opportunity for start-ups who have limited start-up capital but still want to get into a lucrative and fulfilling business. Start by assessing your passion and skills to decide what kind of workshops or classes you want to offer. Whether you choose the arts, dance or yoga, each area offers unique opportunities to reach people and be an asset at events.

Preparation requires only minimal equipment. For example, art workshops require basic painting equipment, while a portable music system is sufficient for dance classes and yoga only requires mats and possibly some tools such as blocks or straps. You can provide these or ask participants to bring their own materials, which can further reduce the initial costs.

An important facet is the location, which should be chosen carefully. Get in touch with the organisers of festivals that attract your target group and negotiate the possibility of offering your services there. It can also be helpful to partner with other local businesses that target similar audiences or offer complementary services.

To publicise your offer, you should use effective marketing strategies. Use digital platforms to generate interest and inform potential participants about your offers. Appealing, informative content and possible early bird discounts can encourage registration and help to create a solid base of participants.

When pricing your courses and workshops, you should remain competitive while covering your costs and making a profit. It is also important to collect feedback after each event to continuously improve your offerings and adapt them to the needs of your customers.

Once you realise that your business is gaining momentum, you might consider adding more course offerings, hiring additional instructors or expanding your services to more events. This can lead to an expansion of your business and allow you to reach a wider audience.

By implementing these steps, you can build a successful presence at festivals that is not only profitable, but also enriches the cultural landscape of the event.

Sustainability services at festivals

If you want to position yourself in the area of sustainability services at festivals, there are many opportunities to make a positive impact while building a business endeavour. This approach involves promoting environmentally friendly practices at events, which not only raises awareness of environmental protection, but also improves the sustainability of the events themselves.

Firstly, you could provide waste collection services aimed at keeping the festival site clean while ensuring that as much waste as possible is recycled. This could include providing separate collection bins for different types of waste, along with a team to ensure that these bins are emptied regularly and sorted correctly. The challenge is to implement efficient collection and sorting procedures that are both practical and cost-effective.

In addition, you could offer the provision of reusable containers as a service. This can range from reusable water bottles sold or loaned to visitors to reusable catering tableware sets. These initiatives help to reduce the use of single-use plastic and promote a more environmentally friendly experience.

Another key aspect of your offer could be advice on organising events according to sustainability principles. Here you would support festival organisers in making their events more environmentally friendly, for example by using energy from renewable sources, minimising water and energy consumption or implementing programmes to offset CO2 emissions.

To successfully market these services, you should build a strong online presence and provide information on social media and your website about the importance of sustainability at events. Education is a key element in driving adoption and participation in your sustainability initiatives. It is also important to work with local environmental groups, non-profit organisations and other stakeholders to increase your credibility and reach.

By introducing standards and best practices for sustainable events, you can establish yourself as a leading provider in the field of sustainability services. This will not only improve your business opportunities, but also make a significant contribution to environmental protection. By actively contributing to reducing the environmental impact of festivals, you will create a positive reputation and promote the growth of your business in an increasingly environmentally conscious market.

The key to success in a low-capital start-up in the event sector lies in the efficient use of resources, creativity and building a solid network. Marketing and word of mouth are particularly important in this sector, so some of your energy should be channelled into building a strong online presence and direct customer contact. The ability to respond flexibly and creatively to customer requests will help you make a name for yourself in the industry.

services

House and pet sitting

Offering house and pet sitting services is an attractive business opportunity for start-ups who want to set up their own business with limited start-up capital. In this day and age, when many people are unable to be at home for extended periods of time due to work or personal commitments, there is a growing demand for trustworthy people to look after homes and pets. Success in this business area depends heavily on the ability to build a high level of trust with customers. This requires not only reliability and a willingness to take on responsibility, but also a deep understanding of the needs of the pets in their care.

To gain a foothold in the house and pet sitting industry, it is first important to familiarise yourself with the basics of pet care and perhaps even invest in pet first aid training. Equally relevant is clarifying legal aspects, such as taking out the right insurance policies and drawing up a standard contract to clearly define mutual duties and responsibilities.

Building a strong, trustworthy brand image is crucial. This can be done by collecting and presenting references, providing a police clearance certificate and creating a professional online presence. A well-designed website and active social media profiles are essential to reach potential customers and give them an insight into the services offered. In addition, word of mouth plays an essential role in the growth of the business, as personal recommendations from satisfied customers are one of the most effective forms of advertising.

Pricing should be carefully considered to be both competitive and profitable. It must reflect the scope and nature of the services provided and may vary depending on the duration of the sitting and any additional services. Building a positive relationship with customers through reliable communication and following all instructions to the letter is another important aspect that leads to customer satisfaction and therefore repeat business.

Continuing education and networking are also important components for long-term success. Keeping up to date with the latest developments in animal care and socialising with other professionals can not only contribute to your own development, but also increase your credibility and professionalism.

By combining in-depth knowledge, reliability and a strong focus on customer relationships, start-ups can build a successful house and pet sitting business that not only provides a valuable service, but is also personally rewarding.

Mobile animal care

The idea of offering a mobile pet grooming service appeals to a growing number of pet owners who are looking for convenient solutions to fulfil the grooming needs of their beloved pets. The advantage of a mobile service is that pets can remain in their familiar surroundings, minimising stress for the animals and providing significant added value for owners. For start-ups without a lot of capital, this service offers an attractive opportunity to enter the pet care market, as the operating costs are often lower compared to stationary facilities.

The key to success in mobile pet grooming lies in the ability to provide a reliable, comfortable and high-quality service. This starts with the purchase or hire of a suitable vehicle to serve as a mobile pet grooming station. Fitting this vehicle with the necessary equipment for pet grooming - from bathing and blow-drying facilities to grooming utensils and possibly even a waiting area for owners - requires careful planning and investment. Despite this initial investment, mobile operations can be more flexible and cost-effective than maintaining a fixed salon location.

Another important component for success is marketing. Developing a strong brand and a clear, engaging marketing plan is crucial to standing out in a competitive market. A professional website that emphasises the uniqueness of your mobile service, along with active social media profiles that provide regular insights into the day-to-day running of your service, can effectively engage potential customers. In addition, word of mouth is particularly valuable in this line of business; satisfied customers who share their positive experiences can be an important source of new business.

Building a good reputation through excellent customer service and the ability to cater to the individual needs of each pet and their owners is also crucial. This includes not only the grooming services themselves, but also the way you interact with the animals and their owners. A friendly, professional demeanour, flexibility in scheduling and a willingness to provide extra service can help build a loyal client base.

For start-ups with a passion for animals and a service-orientated attitude, a mobile pet grooming service offers an excellent opportunity to start a fulfilling and profitable business. Through a combination of high quality service, effective marketing and a strong focus on customer relationships, you can successfully establish and grow in this field.

Plant care and advice

Providing plant care and consultancy services is an excellent business idea for start-ups with a green thumb who want to turn their passion for plants into a profitable business. At a time when awareness of the positive effects of plants on well-being and indoor air quality is increasing, there is a growing demand for plant care expertise from both private individuals and companies who want to make their working environments more natural.

Such a shop can focus on providing personalised advice to help customers choose the right plants for their specific needs and room conditions. This includes taking into account not only the light, humidity and space, but also the care requirements and aesthetic preferences of the customer. Developing customised care plans that include clear instructions on watering, fertilising and general care can help customers keep their plants healthy and attractive in the long term.

For companies that want to beautify their office space with living plants, a comprehensive service can be offered, ranging from the selection of suitable plants to regular care and advice in the event of problems. This provides a continuous source of income and strengthens customer relationships through regular interaction.

Success in this business area depends heavily on the ability to build trust and establish yourself as an expert in the field of plant care. Creating informational materials, such as care guides or blog posts on various plant topics, can help demonstrate expertise and attract customers to the service. A strong online presence, including a professional website and active social media channels, is essential to reach the target audience and market the service.

Networking and word of mouth also play an important role in customer acquisition. Collaborating with local nurseries, interior design shops or coworking spaces can provide opportunities to reach new customers and establish partnerships. Satisfied customers who share their positive experience are often the best advertisement for the service.

For start-ups ready to enter this growing field, the plant care and consulting industry offers an exciting opportunity to start a business that can not only be financially rewarding, but also provide the opportunity to impact people's work and living spaces in a positive way. With the right mix of expertise, marketing strategy and customer service, you can build a successful plant care and consulting business.

IoT solutions (Internet of Things)

The development of IoT (Internet of Things) solutions for smart homes, intelligent cities or industrial applications represents a forward-looking business idea that has the potential to fundamentally change the way we live and work. IoT technology enables the networking and control of devices via the internet, leading to more efficient, energy-efficient and intelligently controlled environments. For start-ups looking to establish themselves in this fast-growing market, the IoT sector offers a wide range of opportunities to develop and offer innovative solutions.

The development of IoT solutions typically involves the creation of hardware, software and the integration of these systems into a functioning unit. In the area of smart homes, these solutions could range from intelligent thermostats and security systems to networked lighting systems, all aimed at increasing home comfort and saving energy. For smart cities, projects could include traffic control systems, smart lighting for public spaces or systems to monitor and improve air quality. In the industrial sector, IoT solutions could contribute to the optimisation of production processes, the remote monitoring of plants or the improvement of logistics.

A successful entry into the IoT business requires both technical and entrepreneurial skills. A basic understanding of electronics, software development and network technologies is just as important as the ability to design market-ready solutions that address real problems. As IoT projects are often complex and involve a wide range of technologies, working with subject matter experts in specific areas or forming a multidisciplinary team can be a key to success.

Marketing IoT solutions requires clear communication of the benefits and added value that your products and services offer. Given the technical nature of IoT, it is crucial to explain to potential customers in an understandable way how your solutions can improve their daily lives or business processes. This can be supported by case studies, demonstrations and customer testimonials.

Another important aspect of building an IoT business is the consideration of security and data protection. As IoT devices often collect and transmit sensitive data, robust security measures must be implemented to gain the trust of users and fulfil regulatory requirements.

For start-ups looking to enter the IoT market, one of the biggest challenges is the rapid development of technology and intense competition. Continuous innovation, the ability to react quickly to market trends and the development of partnerships with other companies can be crucial to gaining an advantage. Despite these challenges, the IoT industry offers tremendous growth potential and the opportunity to be at the forefront of a technological revolution that will shape our society and economy in the years to come.

Virtual interior design

Virtual interior design offers an innovative business idea that has great potential, especially in today's digitally connected world. By providing consultancy services to help customers design and remodel their living or working spaces virtually, start-ups without extensive start-up capital can fill a niche that is both practical and increasingly in demand. This service appeals to a broad target group, including those looking for a cost-effective way to redesign their spaces without the physical presence of a designer.

The core of virtual interior design lies in the use of digital technologies to create and visualise design concepts. Clients can submit photos and measurements of their rooms online, whereupon the interior designer creates detailed designs and 3D visualisations using specialised software. These approaches allow clients to view different design options and make changes before any physical changes are made. This process saves time and money and minimises the risk of design errors.

A key advantage of virtual interior design is the flexibility it offers both customers and service providers. Customers can access services on demand, regardless of geographical restrictions, while service providers can operate their business from virtually anywhere. This flexibility, coupled with the ability to reach customers via social media and online marketing, makes virtual interior design an attractive option for start-ups.

To be successful, virtual interior designers must not only have excellent design skills and a good understanding of spatial design, but also be competent in the use of design software and 3D visualisation tools. In addition, a deep understanding of current design trends and customer needs is required to provide customised solutions that meet or exceed customer expectations.

Creating a strong online presence, including a professionally designed website and active social media accounts, is essential to promote the services to a wider audience. The website should include a gallery of previous projects, client reviews and detailed information about the services offered. Social media platforms can be used to share design ideas, offer interior design tips and encourage direct interactions with potential clients.

Virtual interior design is not only a business idea with low barriers to entry, but also offers the opportunity to be creative and make a visible impact on people's living and working spaces. By combining technical skills, creative talent and effective marketing, start-ups in this field can build a successful and satisfying business.

Voice services

Offering language services that go beyond translation and include services such as editing, proofreading or content writing in different languages is a great business idea, especially in our increasingly globalised world. Companies looking to expand their reach into international markets often face the challenge of ensuring that their communications are not only linguistically accurate, but also culturally appropriate and relevant to their target audiences. There are many opportunities here for language experts who have the necessary knowledge and skills to provide high quality language services.

The demand for such services is high and spans a wide range of industries including, but not limited to, technology, law, medicine, education and media. In addition to the ability to produce accurate and culturally sensitive translations, providing editing and proofreading services requires a deep understanding of the nuances of the target and source language, as well as the ability to edit texts so that they have a clear and coherent style and are free of grammatical and spelling errors. Content writing also requires creativity and the ability to write engaging, target audience-appropriate copy that effectively conveys the client's message.

A key aspect of building a successful language services business is specialisation. By focussing on specific languages, industries or service types, you can establish yourself as an expert in your field and set yourself apart from the competition. This also allows you to develop in-depth knowledge and specific skills that are of particular value to your target customers.

Digitalisation has also made it easier to offer language services on a global scale. A strong online presence, including a professional website and active profiles on social media platforms or specialised portals, is crucial to reach potential clients and showcase your service offering. Client reviews and recommendations can help build trust with potential clients and emphasise the quality of your work.

Networking and building relationships with other professionals in related fields, such as graphic design, web development or marketing, can also be valuable, as these often require complementary services that you can offer in conjunction with your language services.

Overall, the provision of voice services offers not only the opportunity to run a profitable business, but also the chance to play a key role in helping companies and organisations to communicate and operate successfully in international markets. With the right skills, a focus on quality and a clear understanding of the needs of your target customers, you can succeed in this dynamic and growing market segment.

Environmental counselling

The provision of environmental consultancy services is a contemporary and increasingly sought-after business idea that reflects the growing global focus on sustainability and environmental protection. For start-ups with expertise in environmental science or sustainable development, environmental consulting offers an excellent opportunity to make a positive contribution to environmental protection while establishing a sustainable business model.

The role of an environmental consultant focuses on helping companies, organisations and individuals to minimise their environmental impact. This can be done through a variety of services, including analysing and optimising energy consumption, developing waste reduction strategies, assisting with the implementation of renewable energy systems and advising on environmental regulatory compliance. In addition, environmental consultants can help their clients set and achieve sustainability targets, which not only benefits the environment but can also have long-term economic benefits for the companies themselves.

An effective way to succeed as an environmental consultant is to develop customised solutions that are specifically tailored to each client's needs and goals. This requires a thorough assessment of the client's current practices, a clear identification of areas where improvements can be made and the development of strategic plans to realise these improvements. It is important to consider the financial, operational and environmental aspects equally in order to promote realistic and sustainable change.

To gain a foothold in this field, it is essential to establish yourself as an expert in your field and gain the trust of potential customers. This can be achieved by building a strong online presence, including a professional website and active social media profiles. Publishing professional articles, attending industry conferences and networking with other professionals can also help to increase your visibility and credibility.

In addition, it is important for environmental consultants to stay abreast of the latest developments in their field. Environmental legislation, energy efficiency technologies and sustainable practices are constantly evolving, and a deep understanding of these changes is critical to providing effective consulting services.

By combining expertise, strategic planning and a strong commitment to environmental protection, environmental consultants can provide a valuable service that improves both environmental sustainability and operational efficiency for their clients. With the increasing global focus on sustainability, environmental consulting offers a promising area of business for motivated and knowledgeable entrepreneurs who want to have a positive impact on the world.

Nutritional counselling and meal prep planning

The provision of nutritional counselling and meal-prep planning services is meeting a growing demand in an increasingly health-conscious society. Many people are looking to improve their eating habits, whether to lose weight, improve physical performance or simply to promote a general sense of well-being. The key to success in this area lies in the ability to offer customised solutions tailored to clients' individual needs, preferences and lifestyles.

As a dietitian or meal prep planner, your role is to share your knowledge of healthy eating and develop practical solutions to help your clients achieve their nutritional goals. This may include creating personalised nutrition plans, meal prep consultations, developing shopping lists and providing healthy recipes. By providing such services, you can help clients establish healthy eating habits that lead to lasting change.

A successful nutritional counselling and meal prep planning business requires not only in-depth knowledge of nutritional science and healthy living, but also excellent communication skills and empathy. The ability to listen and customise individual plans is crucial, as each client has unique needs and challenges. In addition, it is important to be motivational and provide ongoing support to help clients stay motivated and achieve their goals.

Building a strong online presence is essential for success in modern nutritional counselling. A professionally designed website that provides detailed information about your services, qualifications and client success stories can appeal to potential clients. Social media platforms are also a great way to promote your services, share valuable content and build a community around healthy eating.

Creating content, such as blog posts, videos and online courses, can further help to demonstrate your expertise and build trust with potential clients. By offering workshops, webinars and public talks, you can expand your network and encourage direct interactions with your target audience.

Nutritional counselling and meal prep planning not only offer the opportunity to run a fulfilling business, but also to make a positive impact on people's health and lives. With commitment, expertise and a customer-centred approach, you can be successful in this field and help raise awareness of the importance of healthy eating.

Food delivery service

The idea of starting a local food delivery service that specialises in delivering food from markets or restaurants that do not offer their own delivery service is particularly attractive for start-ups without significant start-up capital. This business model offers a pragmatic solution to fill a gap in the market while starting with relatively low barriers to entry. The key to success lies in careful planning, the identification of a suitable target group and the efficient utilisation of available resources.

Firstly, it is important to conduct market research to understand the need and interest for such a service in the local community. This could be done by conducting surveys, analysing competitor offerings and studying consumer trends. A deep understanding of the target audience, such as working families, the elderly, or people without access to transport, is crucial to developing a successful business model.

One critical aspect is minimising the initial investment. As the idea is designed for start-ups without large amounts of capital, you should consider how you can utilise existing resources. For example, the delivery service could initially be launched with your own vehicle or by using bicycles in urban areas. Co-operation with markets or restaurants could also be an option in order to share advertising costs or even negotiate a commission for each customer generated by the delivery service.

Technology also offers cost-effective ways to efficiently organise the service and reach customers. A simple but well-designed website or mobile app can simplify the ordering process for customers. Initially, existing platforms such as WhatsApp, Facebook Messenger or email could be used for orders to reduce development costs. Social media channels are also an effective and inexpensive way to raise awareness of the service and build a customer community.

Networking and partnerships are essential. Establishing relationships with local shops and restaurants that could benefit from your delivery service is a win-win situation. These businesses get an additional source of revenue and advertising, while your service can benefit from their existing customer base. It's also important to build a good relationship with end customers to create a loyal customer base and generate positive word of mouth.

Flexibility and adaptability are also key. The market and consumer preferences can change quickly, so it is important to be open to feedback and adapt the service accordingly. This could mean expanding the delivery offering, introducing additional services such as online payments or special delivery options.

To summarise, starting a local food delivery service is a viable business idea for start-ups without large amounts of capital. Through careful planning, utilising modern technology and building strong local partnerships, you can offer a vital service that has the potential to grow and succeed. The challenge lies in the execution and ongoing commitment to continuously improve and customise the service to meet the needs of customers.

Photography

Using photography as a business idea can be a rewarding endeavour for those with a good camera and a keen eye for detail. This field offers numerous opportunities, from event photography to portrait sessions to product photography, with each of these segments bringing its own challenges and rewards. The key to success lies in the ability to stand out and find a niche that both reflects your passion and meets a demand in the market.

Firstly, it is important to define your own skills and what you offer. Event photography, including weddings, birthdays and corporate events, requires the ability to capture meaningful moments in often hectic environments. Portrait sessions, whether for individuals, families or pets, require a good understanding of light, composition and the ability to interact with clients on a personal level to best capture their personality. Product photography, on the other hand, requires an eye for detail and the ability to present objects in a way that emphasises their best features and appeals to potential buyers.

Developing a unique style is crucial. In a saturated market, your individual style can be what sets you apart from the competition. Whether through the way you use light, design your compositions or handle post-production, your unique style becomes your calling card.

A solid online presence is essential. A professionally designed website that showcases your portfolio is crucial to attracting potential customers. Complemented by a strong presence on social media platforms such as Instagram, Facebook and Pinterest, you can reach a wider audience and expand your network. Sharing behind-the-scenes footage, client reviews and personal projects can help build a connection with your audience.

Networking should not be underestimated. Building relationships with other service providers in the event industry, such as event planners, caterers and florists, can lead to referrals. Similarly, working with local product photography companies is a great way to expand your service offering.

Customer relationships are the key to long-term success. Satisfied customers will not only lead to repeat business, but also generate valuable referrals. It is therefore important to provide excellent customer service, from the initial enquiry to the delivery of the final images.

Ultimately, continuous training is essential. Photography is a rapidly evolving field, and it's important to stay on top of the latest technology and creative trends. Workshops, online courses and specialised literature can help sharpen your skills and learn new techniques.

To summarise, photography offers a fascinating opportunity for creatives to turn their passion into a profitable business. With the right equipment, a unique style and a customer retention strategy, you can succeed in this dynamic field.

Language lessons

Offering language tuition, whether face-to-face or online, is an excellent business idea for those who are fluent in one or more foreign languages. This service is in ever-increasing demand due to globalisation and the growing importance of multilingualism in many areas of life. Successful language teaching combines pedagogical skill with modern technologies and methods to provide learners with an effective and engaging educational experience.

The first step is to define your offer. Decide which languages and levels you want to teach and whether you specialise in certain areas such as business language, conversation or exam preparation. Specialisation can help you stand out in a saturated market and target customers who have specific learning goals.

The choice between face-to-face and online teaching depends on several factors, including your preferences, target audience and geographical considerations. Online teaching offers flexibility and the ability to reach students worldwide, while face-to-face teaching allows for deeper interactions and more direct feedback. Many teachers combine both approaches to cover a wider range of learning needs.

Technology plays a crucial role in modern language teaching. Platforms such as Zoom, Skype or specialised language learning apps offer a wide range of possibilities for online teaching, including video calls, interactive exercises and the use of digital teaching materials. Developing or customising your own teaching materials tailored to the needs and interests of your students can significantly increase learning success.

Marketing your language course is crucial to attracting students. A professional website that clearly presents your offer is essential. Complement this with an active presence on social media and platforms that specialise in language teaching and tutoring. Word of mouth, especially from satisfied students, is one of the most effective forms of advertising, so excellent tuition should always be a priority.

Networking with other language teachers and educational institutions can also be beneficial. It provides opportunities for co-operation, sharing best practices and even referrals. Further training in pedagogical methods and language didactics is also important to ensure that your teaching remains up-to-date and effective.

Offering language lessons can be very fulfilling and provides the opportunity to support people in their pursuit of multilingualism and intercultural competence. With the right mix of expertise, teaching skills and marketing, you can build a successful career as a language teacher, whether face-to-face, online or both.

Babysitting and childcare

Starting a babysitting or childcare service is a business idea that requires not only a lot of heart and commitment, but also a strong love of working with children. If you are in the fortunate position of having patience and a caring nature, a world of opportunities opens up to you where the demand for quality childcare is constantly growing. The key to success in this field is to build trust and establish a network that grows through positive experiences and referrals from your clients.

Firstly, you should familiarise yourself with the necessary qualifications and certificates that underline your competence and reliability. These usually include first aid courses specifically for children, child protection certificates and possibly other qualifications in early childhood education. These certificates are not only reassuring for parents, but also increase your confidence in your abilities.

Building a trustworthy reputation plays a central role. Satisfied parents and children are the best ambassadors for your service. By acting reliably, professionally and warmly from the outset, you lay the foundations for successful word-of-mouth advertising that will drive your business forward in the long term. This presupposes that you always have an open ear for the needs and wishes of families and that you respond flexibly to them.

Marketing is also a crucial factor in the success of your babysitting or childcare service. A well-designed website and social media presence are now essential to raise awareness and attract new customers. In addition, participating in local events and networking with schools and nurseries can help to promote your service to a wider audience.

In order to hold your own in a highly competitive market, it can make sense to offer additional services. These could include tutoring, creative workshops or language tuition, for example, which raise your profile and increase the value of your offering. Diversifying your range of services makes you more attractive to a broader target group and can lead to stable customer demand.

Another important aspect is ensuring the safety and well-being of the children. It is of utmost importance to create a safe and stimulating environment where children feel comfortable and secure. Establishing clear guidelines and contingency plans, as well as open and transparent communication with parents, goes a long way to cementing trust and building long-term relationships.

After all, continuous professional development is a must in the dynamic world of childcare. By regularly informing yourself about new pedagogical methods and trends and undergoing further training, you not only ensure the quality of your services, but also increase your attractiveness as a provider.

In sum, starting a babysitting or childcare service provides an excellent opportunity to turn your passion for working with children into a fulfilling and profitable business. By building a trustworthy reputation, thoughtful marketing, expanding your offerings, and a strong commitment to children's safety and education, you can build a successful career in this enriching field.

Garden maintenance and landscaping

The business idea of garden maintenance and landscaping is particularly attractive for start-ups with limited capital who are prepared to do physical labour and react flexibly to weather conditions. This sector offers a variety of services, from simple lawn care to complex outdoor landscaping, and appeals to a wide range of customers. Entry into this business can be achieved with a manageable investment in basic gardening equipment, and the potential for growth and expansion is considerable.

To begin with, it is important to have a clear idea of the services on offer. Basic services include lawn mowing, weed removal, hedge trimming and general garden maintenance. Depending on skills and interests, other specialised services such as landscaping, irrigation system installation or seasonal gardening can be added. The ability to offer a wide range of services can increase the appeal of your business to different customers and help to attract customers.

A decisive factor for success in this business is the ability to work efficiently and regardless of weather conditions. This requires a certain degree of flexibility in planning and a willingness to work in less than ideal conditions if necessary. At the same time, it is important to ensure safety and well-being at work by wearing appropriate protective clothing and paying attention to weather warnings.

Purchasing the necessary gardening tools is the initial investment. A few basic tools such as a lawn mower, hedge trimmer, shovels and gloves are often enough to get you started. As time goes on and the business grows, more specialised tools and equipment can be added to work more efficiently and offer additional services.

Marketing and customer acquisition are other important aspects. Word of mouth is particularly valuable in this business, and satisfied customers can be an important source of new orders. A professional presence on the internet, whether through a dedicated website or social media channels, can also help to publicise the business and engage with potential customers. Local advertising, flyers and networking in the community can be other effective ways to attract attention.

Building a good reputation through reliable, high-quality work is crucial. Customers are looking for service providers they can trust to come into their gardens and meet or exceed their expectations. A willingness to listen to customer needs and offer customised solutions can help build long-term relationships and create a loyal customer base.

Overall, garden maintenance and landscaping offers an excellent opportunity for start-ups with limited capital to create a business with growth potential. Through hard work, a flexible approach and a focus on customer satisfaction, this line of business can not only generate a steady income, but also provide a fulfilling career for those with a passion for outdoor work and landscaping.

Dropshipping

Dropshipping is an attractive business idea for start-ups, especially for those who want to start with limited capital and have a strong interest in e-commerce and marketing. This method of selling online allows you to offer products without having to buy them in advance or physically store them. Instead, you work with a supplier who ships the products directly to your customers as soon as a sale is made. The key to success in dropshipping lies in effective marketing, careful selection of products and suppliers, and excellent customer service.

At its core, dropshipping requires a good knowledge of e-commerce and the ability to identify market niches and trends. You create an online shop, select products that you want to sell and advertise these products. When a customer buys from your shop, you buy the product from the supplier, who then ships it directly to the customer. Your profit margin is the difference between the sales price you set and the price the supplier charges.

One of the first challenges is selecting trustworthy suppliers with high-quality products. Platforms such as AliExpress, Oberlo or SaleHoo can make it easier to get started by providing access to thousands of suppliers. It is crucial to carefully vet suppliers to ensure they are reliable and the products match the descriptions. Equally important is selecting products that fulfil a demand, have little direct competition and promise good margins.

Marketing is at the heart of the dropshipping business. Digital marketing, including search engine optimisation (SEO), paid advertising (e.g. Google Ads, Facebook Ads), email marketing and the use of social media, is crucial to drive traffic to your online shop and generate sales. Content marketing through blogs or YouTube channels can also help attract potential customers and build trust in your brand.

As you do not have direct control over shipping and logistics, outstanding customer service is crucial to ensure customer trust and satisfaction. This includes quick responses to customer enquiries, transparent communication about shipping times and conditions, and a clear returns policy. The ability to respond quickly and efficiently to problems with orders can help avoid negative customer reviews and increase customer loyalty.

Dropshipping offers the opportunity to scale without the need for significant upfront investment in stock. As your business grows, you can expand your product offering, invest in improved marketing and potentially even develop your own branded products. Flexibility and adaptability to changing market trends and customer preferences are crucial to long-term success.

Overall, dropshipping offers an exciting opportunity for start-ups to enter the world of e-commerce without the usual risks and costs associated with setting up a traditional retail business. With strategic planning, a focus on marketing and customer service, and a constant willingness to learn and adapt, you can build and operate a profitable dropshipping business.

Equipment hire

The business idea of renting out equipment that is not in constant use is proving to be an excellent opportunity for founders with limited capital. This model is based on the efficient utilisation of existing resources - be it high-quality camera equipment, DJ equipment or camping supplies - and transforms them into a potential source of income. The key to success in this business lies in the ability to keep the products in perfect condition, develop a deep understanding of market demand and establish a smooth, customer-friendly rental process.

In order to start renting out equipment, a thorough market analysis is essential. It is important to find out which types of equipment are particularly in demand and which target groups are most likely to make use of the offer. Demand can be seasonal or influenced by current trends, which requires flexibility in adapting the offer. The condition of the equipment plays a crucial role in success, as customers expect the rented items not only to work, but also to be well-maintained and clean.

Marketing for the rental services should include both digital and traditional channels to reach a broad target group. A professionally designed website that clearly presents the offer and simplifies the booking process is just as important as a presence on social media to engage with potential customers and share special offers or news. Local advertising measures, such as flyers or partnerships with event planners and other local companies, can generate additional attention.

To manage rentals, it is advisable to set up an efficient system that monitors bookings, availability and equipment condition. This not only helps to keep track and avoid double bookings, but also guarantees customers a smooth process from the first contact to the return of the equipment. Such a system should be flexible enough to respond to customer requests and transparent in terms of costs, rental conditions and liability issues.

Excellent customer service is the backbone of a successful rental business. This includes not only providing guidance on how to use the equipment correctly and responding quickly to enquiries or problems, but also collecting and acting on customer feedback. A satisfied customer is a potential repeat customer and can contribute significantly to the growth of the business through positive word of mouth.

Over time, equipment hire provides opportunities to scale and expand the offering. Based on customer experience and feedback, additional services or new equipment can be added to further develop the business and expand the customer base. However, the basis for success always lies in the quality of the offering, the reliability of the service and the ability to adapt to the changing needs of the market.

Domestic help and cleaning service

Starting a home and office cleaning service is an accessible business opportunity that can begin with minimal investment, especially if you choose to utilise your clients' cleaning supplies and equipment first. This approach allows founders to focus on acquiring clients and providing quality services without having to worry about the initial cost of equipment right away.

A successful cleaning service is built on trust, reliability and customer satisfaction. The basis for this is the quality of the work you do. Customers expect their premises to be spotless after every cleaning, which means that attention to detail and a systematic approach to cleaning are essential. In addition, the ability to adapt to the specific needs and preferences of each customer plays a major role in customer satisfaction and retention.

To get started with your cleaning service, you should begin with a thorough market analysis and a solid business plan. Understand local demand and identify your target customers, whether they are busy families, single people or businesses looking to maintain their office space. Clearly positioning your service as trustworthy, efficient and flexible can help you stand out from other providers.

Promoting your cleaning service can be done through word of mouth, local advertising, using social media and setting up a simple but informative website. The aim is to increase your visibility and inform potential customers about your services, prices and special offers. A professional image, both online and in direct customer communication, helps to build a positive first impression.

A particular challenge when running a cleaning service is logistics, especially scheduling and route optimisation in order to use time and resources efficiently. Flexible planning that takes into account both the needs of customers and your own capacities is crucial to the smooth running of your business. A willingness to collect and respond to feedback is also important to continuously improve your service and build a positive customer relationship.

During the initial stages, when you may be using clients' equipment and cleaning supplies, it is important to communicate clearly what is needed and ensure that you can work effectively with the materials provided. This can also serve as a temporary measure while you accumulate capital to purchase your own materials and equipment that will allow you to expand and improve your services.

To summarise, starting a home and office cleaning service is a viable business idea with little initial investment that can focus on long-term growth and developing a loyal customer base. The key to success lies in providing a reliable, high-quality service that caters to the individual needs of customers, coupled with effective marketing and a strong focus on customer satisfaction.

Private tuition

Offering tutoring services is a great way to monetise your knowledge and skills in a particular subject area. This service can benefit both pupils and students and can be organised flexibly - in person or via online platforms. This flexibility makes tutoring particularly attractive as it can adapt to both the teacher's lifestyle and the learner's needs.

The first step to successfully launching a tutoring service is to identify your area of specialisation and assess the demand in that area. Whether it's maths, languages, science or humanities, each discipline has its own audience. The key is to choose a specialism in which you not only have in-depth knowledge and experience, but also a passion for teaching.

Once you have determined your specialism, it is important to develop a strategy for the delivery of your service. Face-to-face tutoring offers the advantage of direct contact and the ability to respond to the learner's immediate needs. However, this form of tutoring can be geographically limited. Online tutoring, on the other hand, offers tremendous flexibility and reach, as you can reach students from different regions or even countries. Thanks to digital technologies such as video conferencing, interactive whiteboards and shared documents, tutor and learner can communicate and collaborate effectively as if they were in the same room.

Clear communication of your offer is crucial to the successful marketing of your tutoring services. Create a profile that highlights your qualifications, experience and the specialism you offer. Use social media, local adverts and online platforms to raise awareness of your services. Many tutors also benefit significantly from word of mouth; satisfied students or their parents can be a valuable source of referrals.

Another important aspect is pricing. Investigate the market to get an understanding of the going rates in your specialism and region. Fair and competitive pricing helps to appeal to a broader range of students while ensuring that your time and expertise are appropriately compensated.

The quality of your tutoring sessions is crucial for long-term success. Commit to your students' success by developing personalised learning plans, providing regular feedback, and continuing professional development in your teaching methods and subject knowledge. The ability to communicate complex concepts clearly and understandably and create a supportive learning environment will not only help improve your students' learning success, but will also enhance your reputation as an excellent tutor.

Overall, offering tutoring services provides a fulfilling way to share your expertise, make a positive impact on the educational journey of others and generate an income at the same time. With the right planning, a clear marketing approach and a commitment to excellence in education, you can build a successful career as a tutor, whether in person or online.

Translation services

Providing translation services opens up a multi-faceted career opportunity for bilingual or multilingual individuals that can benefit both organisations and individuals. The range of services in this field is broad and can range from the written translation of documents to oral interpreting services at events. This spectrum allows translators to specialise in certain niches or types of translation, depending on their skills, interests and the needs of the market.

The first step for aspiring translators is to assess their language skills and specialised knowledge. Proficiency in more than one language is essential, but equally important is an understanding of cultural nuances and jargon common to certain industries. Many translators therefore choose to specialise in certain fields such as law, medicine, engineering or business, making their services more valuable to specific target audiences.

To be successful as a translator, it is crucial to build a solid portfolio and establish a strong online presence. A professional website that showcases your services, specialisations and previous work can be an effective tool to attract new clients. In addition, you can register on freelancer platforms or with professional translator associations to increase your visibility and gain credibility.

Networking plays an important role in the world of translation. Attending industry-specific conferences, workshops and other events can not only sharpen your skills, but also provide you with valuable contacts to potential clients and colleagues. Word of mouth from satisfied clients can also be a powerful tool to grow your business.

For translators specialising in interpreting services, the ability to communicate accurately and clearly under pressure is essential. Interpreting at events, conferences or in sensitive situations such as negotiations or medical consultations requires not only linguistic competence, but also a deep understanding of the subject matter and excellent interpersonal skills.

An important aspect that is often overlooked is the importance of professionalism and ethical standards in the translation industry. Discretion and confidentiality are particularly important as translators often work with sensitive information. Handling this information with confidence is crucial to building long-term relationships with clients.

To summarise, translation services offer an exciting career opportunity for multilingual individuals who want to turn their language skills into a professional offering. With the right mix of expertise, marketing strategy and networking skills, you can build a successful career in the translation industry that brings not only financial but also intellectual and cultural rewards. The demand for high quality translations is constantly growing as the world becomes more interconnected, making this field an attractive and potentially lucrative career path.

Art hire and sale

Art rental and sales, which puts local artists front and centre, offers a unique opportunity to make art more accessible while helping artists earn an income. This business model creates a win-win situation for artists and art lovers alike by providing a platform to showcase artwork to a wider audience. Businesses and private households are given the opportunity to liven up their spaces with unique artworks without having to make a long-term commitment, while artists can increase their reach and tap into new revenue streams.

The key to success in this business lies in the careful selection of artworks and building a diverse collection that appeals to different tastes and budgets. It is important to work closely with the artists not only to develop an understanding of their work, but also to reach fair agreements that benefit both parties. This often involves negotiating terms such as loan fees, sale prices and the length of loan periods.

To start such a business, a passion for art and a deep understanding of the local art market is essential. Networking events, art exhibitions and local artist workshops are ideal places to socialise and build a relationship with artists. At the same time, it is important to cultivate relationships with potential clients by emphasising the benefits of art rental, such as the ability to regularly refresh the aesthetics of a space or test artworks before making a purchase.

Marketing plays a crucial role in promoting the art rental and sales business. A professional website that showcases both the artworks available and information about the artists involved can be an effective platform for generating interest and attracting customers. Social media channels also offer the opportunity to regularly present new works and announce events or exhibitions that can attract potential customers.

Another important aspect is customer service, particularly advice on the selection of artworks and support with logistical issues such as transporting and installing the works. A personalised approach that caters to the specific needs and preferences of each customer can help build long-term relationships and generate word of mouth.

To summarise, art rental and sale offers a fascinating business opportunity that not only promotes the accessibility of art, but also supports local artists. By creating a platform that makes artworks accessible to a wider audience, this business model can help foster a vibrant local art scene while generating a sustainable income for artists. With the right approach and commitment, art rental and sales can become an enriching endeavour that brings art and community together in a meaningful way.

Specialised cleaning services

Art rental and sales, which puts local artists front and centre, offers a unique opportunity to make art more accessible while helping artists earn an income. This business model creates a win-win situation for artists and art lovers alike by providing a platform to showcase artwork to a wider audience. Businesses and private households are given the opportunity to liven up their spaces with unique artworks without having to make a long-term commitment, while artists can increase their reach and tap into new revenue streams.

The key to success in this business lies in the careful selection of artworks and building a diverse collection that appeals to different tastes and budgets. It is important to work closely with the artists not only to develop an understanding of their work, but also to reach fair agreements that benefit both parties. This often involves negotiating terms such as loan fees, sale prices and the length of loan periods.

To start such a business, a passion for art and a deep understanding of the local art market is essential. Networking events, art exhibitions and local artist workshops are ideal places to socialise and build a relationship with artists. At the same time, it is important to cultivate relationships with potential clients by emphasising the benefits of art rental, such as the ability to regularly refresh the aesthetics of a space or test artworks before making a purchase.

Marketing plays a crucial role in promoting the art rental and sales business. A professional website that showcases both the artworks available and information about the artists involved can be an effective platform for generating interest and attracting customers. Social media channels also offer the opportunity to regularly present new works and announce events or exhibitions that can attract potential customers.

Another important aspect is customer service, particularly advice on the selection of artworks and support with logistical issues such as transporting and installing the works. A personalised approach that caters to the specific needs and preferences of each customer can help build long-term relationships and generate word of mouth.

To summarise, art rental and sale offers a fascinating business opportunity that not only promotes the accessibility of art, but also supports local artists. By creating a platform that makes artworks accessible to a wider audience, this business model can help foster a vibrant local art scene while generating a sustainable income for artists. With the right approach and commitment, art rental and sales can become an enriching endeavour that brings art and community together in a meaningful way.

Personal development and life counselling

Establishing a business in coaching for career development, lifestyle or personal growth is an attractive option, especially for start-ups with limited capital. These industries primarily require a deep understanding of human behaviour, excellent communication skills and the ability to help others achieve their goals, rather than substantial financial investment.

An essential first step is to invest in your own education. There are a variety of courses and certifications available online that can increase both your knowledge and credibility in your chosen field. Although these require some investment, the cost is relatively low compared to many other endeavours.

Another important aspect is specialising in a specific niche market in which you have particular knowledge or experience. This specialisation helps you to stand out from the competition and address your target group more effectively. By positioning yourself as an expert in a specific field, you can gain the trust of potential clients.

Building a strong personal brand is also crucial. A professional online presence supported by a website, social media and networking platforms can help you promote your business and build trust with your target clients. Producing quality content that demonstrates your expertise and commitment to your clients' personal growth plays a central role in this.

Networking is an essential part of building a successful coaching business. By attending industry events and participating in professional groups, you can make valuable connections and introduce your services to a wider audience. Utilising digital platforms for networking provides additional opportunities to expand your reach and connect with potential clients.

Flexible pricing can be helpful in the beginning to attract a broader clientele and build long-term customer relationships. Discounts or special introductory offers can incentivise prospective customers to try out your services.

Positive customer reviews are a powerful tool to gain the trust of potential new customers. Encourage satisfied clients to share their experiences to make it easier for others to decide in favour of your services.

Finally, it is important to understand the legal aspects of your business and ensure that you have taken all the necessary steps to register and secure your business. Data protection, contract law and any insurance that may be required are key points here.

The key to success in the coaching industry is the ability to create real change in people's lives. Through ongoing training, building a strong brand and creating positive client experiences, you can establish yourself as a valued coach in your field.

Leisure activities and workshops

As a start-up entrepreneur who wants to organise local workshops or activities in areas such as yoga, meditation, arts and crafts or cooking, you face an exciting and rewarding challenge. This type of business not only offers the opportunity to share your passion with others, but can also create a sustainable source of income. To be successful, it is important to be strategic and focus on creating value for your participants.

Firstly, it is crucial to understand your target audience. Think about who might be interested in your workshops or activities and what their specific needs and interests are. This understanding will help you to develop customised offers that provide real added value.

Choosing the right location plays an important role. Not only should the location be easily accessible for your target group, but it should also offer an atmosphere that suits the theme of the workshop. For yoga or meditation courses, for example, a quiet, relaxing environment is ideal, while cookery courses require a well-equipped kitchen.

Marketing and advertising are essential to attract participants to your workshops. Use social media, local community boards and word of mouth to promote your events. An engaging, informative website or landing page that provides details about your workshops, background and registration options can also be very effective.

It's also important to carefully plan your attendees' experience. This includes not only the structure of the workshop itself, but also small details that can make a big difference, such as welcoming participants, providing snacks or drinks, and following up with additional resources or feedback opportunities.

In addition, partnering with local businesses or organisations that target similar audiences can be an effective way to expand your reach and attract new participants. These partnerships can include cross-promotional activities, sponsored events or simply reciprocal referrals.

The pricing of your workshops requires careful consideration. Not only do you need to cover the costs of organising and running the workshops, you also need to make a profit. At the same time, it is important to set prices that are attractive and affordable for your target group. Thorough market research can help you find a balance.

Ultimately, building a community around your workshops can ensure long-term success. Encourage interaction between participants and create opportunities for them to stay in touch outside of the workshops. This can be done through online forums, regular meetings or membership programmes.

By carefully planning and implementing these elements, you can build a successful business that is not only financially rewarding, but also has a positive impact on the lives of your participants.

Virtual property assistance

The idea of offering virtual assistance services specifically for the real estate sector is an excellent business opportunity for start-ups who want to use their skills in organisation, communication and data analysis. The property sector is dynamic and requires its players, agents and managers to manage a variety of tasks efficiently. A virtual property assistant can provide valuable support by taking over routine tasks and allowing professionals to focus on selling and looking after their clients.

The first step to establishing yourself as a virtual property assistant is to understand the specific needs and challenges faced by property professionals. These include not only administrative tasks such as appointment scheduling and customer care, but also specialised services such as managing property listings, preparing market analyses, maintaining customer relationships and supporting contract processing.

A key factor for success in this area is the ability to build trusting relationships with your clients. This requires not only excellent communication skills and a high degree of reliability, but also a deep understanding of the property sector. Further training courses and certifications in property management can not only increase your expertise, but also strengthen the trust of potential clients in your services.

Technology plays a crucial role in virtual assistance. Knowledge of relevant software and platform solutions, such as CRM (Customer Relationship Management) systems, MLS (Multiple Listing Service) and market analysis tools, is essential. Equally important is the ability to communicate and work effectively remotely, which requires a solid internet connection and mastery of communication and project management tools.

Marketing and networking are crucial to publicising your services. A professional website that showcases your services, qualifications and success stories is essential. You should also have an active presence on social media and platforms where property professionals hang out. Making contacts by attending industry events, both online and offline, can open more doors.

The pricing of your services requires careful consideration. Not only should it reflect the quality and scope of your services, but it should also be competitive. One option is to offer different packages tailored to the different needs and budgets of your customers.

Ultimately, specialising in niche areas within the property sector, such as luxury properties, commercial properties or specific geographical areas, can help to establish yourself as an expert in a particular segment and gain a clear competitive advantage.

As a virtual property assistant, you not only provide valuable support for your clients, but also help to make their business more efficient and successful. With the right combination of expertise, technological skills and marketing strategy, you can occupy a niche that is in demand and build a thriving business.

Virtual event planning

The increasing popularity of online events offers a unique business opportunity for start-ups with organisational skills and knowledge of how to use online event platforms. Planning and organising virtual events, webinars or workshops requires not only an understanding of the technological side, but also of the dynamics of participant interaction in a digital space. This is about creating valuable and engaging experiences for participants while effectively supporting the organiser's objectives.

To begin with, it is important to identify a niche in which you would like to offer your services. Selecting a specific target audience or type of event can help you offer customised solutions and stand out from the competition. Whether it's educational workshops, networking events, product launches or entertainment offerings, each type of event requires a unique approach to planning and execution.

Technical equipment plays a central role in this business model. A thorough knowledge of various online event platforms such as Zoom, Webex, Microsoft Teams or specialised event management systems is essential. This includes not only the ability to run the event technically flawlessly, but also the knowledge of how to effectively utilise interactive elements such as polls, Q&A sessions, breakout rooms and virtual networking opportunities.

In addition, the successful implementation of online events requires strong organisational skills. This includes precise planning of the event schedule, coordination with speakers or presenters, managing registrations and participant data and ensuring smooth communication before, during and after the event. Another important aspect is marketing and promoting the event to ensure broad participation. The use of social media, email marketing and other digital channels is central to this.

A successful service provider in this area not only offers technical support, but also acts as a consultant for the content of the event. This includes developing strategies to increase participant interaction, advising on the selection of topics and speakers, optimising the event agenda and creating follow-up measures to maximise the long-term value of the event.

To be successful in this industry, it is important to build a strong brand and online presence. A professional website that showcases your services, experiences and success stories can help to convince potential customers. Similarly, recommendations and testimonials from satisfied customers can go a long way in building credibility and trust.

Offering services for the planning and realisation of virtual events opens up a wide range of possibilities. With the right mix of technical know-how, creative thinking and effective project management, you can become a valuable resource for companies and organisations looking to expand their reach in the digital world.

Creative writing and ghostwriting

In the field of creative writing and ghostwriting, there are many opportunities for start-ups, especially in times when the demand for high-quality, authentic content continues to grow. This sector is characterised by a high demand for individual, creative solutions, ranging from the creation of unique books and the writing of appealing blog posts to the conception of convincing speeches and presentations. Whether it's helping organisations with their content strategy or helping individuals tell their personal stories, creative writers can play a key role in bringing ideas to life and creating content that really resonates.

Success in this field relies heavily on the ability to market yourself effectively and find a niche where you can utilise your particular skills and interests. Specialising in certain types of content or industries can help to position yourself as an expert and attract the attention of potential clients. It's also important to build a strong portfolio that reflects the breadth and depth of your skills to build trust and credibility with your target customers.

A professional appearance, be it through a well-designed website, a meaningful LinkedIn profile or clear communication with customers, is crucial to being taken seriously in the industry. At the same time, success in this field requires a willingness to continually learn and develop in order to keep pace with the ever-changing demands of the market.

Networking and relationship building are also essential to secure business and establish a base of loyal customers. The ability to work effectively remotely and master the technological tools required to collaborate with clients and manage projects is more important than ever in today's digitalised world.

Although competition from artificial intelligence and automated writing tools is increasing, the human ability to convey complex ideas, create emotional depth and communicate with readers on a personal level remains irreplaceable. For startups willing to take on these challenges, the creative writing and ghostwriting sector offers a rich landscape of opportunities to turn their passion for writing into a successful business.

Content Creation

The role of a content creator has evolved into a versatile and potentially lucrative career option in the digital era. People who create content in the form of videos, blogs or podcasts use platforms such as YouTube, WordPress or Spotify to reach and grow their audience. The income opportunities in this area are diverse and range from advertising revenue to sponsored content and subscriptions.

The successful career of a content creator begins with identifying a target audience and developing a clear understanding of what content might appeal to them and offer added value. Authenticity and passion for the chosen topic are crucial as they form the basis of a strong bond with the audience. This relationship is key to building a loyal community that regularly consumes and supports content.

Creating high-quality content requires not only creativity and expertise in the chosen field, but also a good understanding of the technical aspects of content production. This includes knowledge of video editing, audio recording, writing and search engine optimisation (SEO). In addition, it is important to be familiar with the algorithms and best practices of the respective platforms in order to maximise the visibility and reach of the content.

Content can be monetised in various ways. Advertising revenue, especially on platforms such as YouTube, is a frequently used source of income where creators are paid for placing adverts before or during their videos. Sponsored content is another way to generate income. Here, companies pay the creator to mention or present their products or services within the content. Subscriptions, for example via platforms such as Patreon, allow fans to directly support their favourite creators, often in exchange for exclusive content or benefits.

In addition to these direct sources of income, there are also indirect opportunities for content creators to generate income, for example through the sale of merchandise, book publications or the organisation of workshops and lectures. Diversifying sources of income is a smart step towards building a sustainable business model and achieving financial stability.

For long-term success, it is essential to build a strong online presence and brand that goes beyond individual platforms. The use of social media to promote content and interact with the community plays an important role in this. It is also important to keep an eye on trends and react flexibly to changes in the digital landscape in order to remain relevant.

To summarise, a career as a content creator offers a creative and fulfilling way to reach and influence an audience. With the right strategy, hard work and the ability to adapt to the ever-changing demands of the digital space, content creators can not only turn their passion into a profession, but also earn a diverse income.

Health and wellness services

The health and wellness sector opens up a wide range of business opportunities for start-ups that cater to people's growing health awareness and individual needs.

Personal training and fitness

Develop personalised training plans and offer personal coaching via video conferencing for customers who want to achieve their fitness goals.

Developing personalised training plans and offering personal coaching via video conferencing is a modern response to the growing demand for flexible and accessible fitness solutions. At a time when people are increasingly looking for ways to improve their health and fitness without having to leave their homes, this service offers an attractive way for customers to achieve their fitness goals.

The key to success in this area lies in personalising and adapting training programmes to the specific needs, abilities and goals of each client. By taking a personalised approach, you can not only create more effective and targeted training plans, but also build a stronger relationship with your clients. This not only boosts their engagement and motivation, but also increases the likelihood of long-term success and customer loyalty.

Using video conferencing technology for coaching allows you to work across geographical boundaries, enabling you to reach a wider audience. During sessions, you can demonstrate exercises, provide feedback on form and technique, make adjustments and offer motivational support. This direct engagement helps replicate the dynamism and effectiveness of face-to-face training, while providing the flexibility that many clients are looking for.

To be successful in this field, it is important to have a sound knowledge of fitness, anatomy and nutrition as well as the ability to develop effective and safe training programmes. It is also beneficial to have strong communication skills and a positive, motivating personality to inspire and motivate clients.

Marketing your services can be done through social media, a professional website, word of mouth and local advertising. A strong online presence that highlights your expertise, client success stories and the unique offering of your coaching can be crucial in attracting potential clients and building trust.

By developing individual training plans and offering personal coaching via video conferencing, you can provide a valuable service that meets today's needs for flexibility, accessibility and personalisation in fitness. With the right combination of expertise, commitment and marketing strategy, you have the opportunity to make a significant impact on the lives of your clients while building a successful online fitness coaching business.

Online fitness courses

Expanding the reach of digital offerings in the fitness industry offers start-ups a promising opportunity to be successful even with limited financial resources. Digitalisation has fundamentally changed the way people exercise and access fitness services. Online fitness courses, from live training sessions to subscription-based training programmes, are opening up new ways to reach a wide audience and build a sustainable business model.

The advantage of digital fitness programmes lies in their flexibility and scalability. Once created, courses and programmes can be made available to an unlimited number of users without incurring additional costs. This differs significantly from traditional gyms, where space is limited and running costs increase with the number of members.

For start-ups with little capital, entering the online fitness market is particularly attractive, as the initial investment is significantly lower compared to physical gyms. The basic requirements only include high-quality equipment for recording training videos, a stable internet connection and a platform on which the courses can be offered. In addition, the effective use of social media and online marketing plays a crucial role in reaching and retaining potential customers.

Live training sessions offer the opportunity to interact directly with participants and foster a sense of community that many people expect from a gym. Real-time communication allows trainers to respond to participants' needs and feedback, resulting in higher customer satisfaction and loyalty.

Subscribable training programmes, on the other hand, offer customers flexibility in terms of when and where they train. Customers can complete the courses according to their individual schedule, which is particularly attractive for those who have a busy work or private life. By providing a variety of classes and programmes tailored to different fitness goals and levels, start-ups can appeal to a wide audience and serve different customer segments.

The challenge in creating online fitness programmes lies in developing high-quality, appealing content that motivates users and retains their loyalty in the long term. This requires not only expertise in the field of fitness, but also knowledge in the areas of video production and online marketing.

To summarise, the market for online fitness classes offers start-ups an attractive opportunity to build and scale a business with little capital. By utilising digital technologies and platforms, they can reach a wide audience and provide a diverse range of training options. However, success in this area requires the ability to create high-quality content, establish a strong online presence and communicate effectively with the target audience.

Nutritional counselling (see above under services)

Educational programmes on various nutrition topics.

The business model based around educational programmes on various nutritional topics offers promising prospects for start-ups, especially if the available equity capital is limited. The key to success in this area is to develop a deep understanding of the needs and preferences of the target group. Careful market research can identify specific areas of interest within nutrition that are particularly in demand. This makes it possible to develop customised educational offerings, which can range from online courses and webinars to e-books and personal consultations.

A key aspect is the design of the content, which should not only be up-to-date and informative, but also appealing and accessible. The integration of multimedia elements such as videos and infographics can significantly enrich the learning experience and increase the attention of the target group. The use of the internet and social media plays a crucial role in the marketing and distribution of these educational programmes. Platforms such as Teachable or Udemy can help to make the courses accessible to a wide audience, while a dedicated website or blog enables a direct connection to customers.

There are many ways to monetise these educational offerings. In addition to the direct sale of courses and materials, subscription models can also be used to generate recurring income. Additional income streams can be generated through affiliate marketing or partnerships with relevant companies in the nutrition sector. To ensure long-term success, it is important to listen to customer feedback and continuously improve the offerings. Building a community and interacting with the target group via social media or special online formats also contributes to customer loyalty and promotes the visibility of the brand.

In this context, it is essential for start-ups to distinguish themselves through high quality, authenticity and sound expertise. With a clear strategy, creative ideas and a focus on the needs of the target group, a successful and sustainable business model can be established in the field of nutrition education, even with limited resources.

Yoga studios and meditation courses

Setting up a yoga studio or offering meditation courses is an attractive business idea for start-ups who want to position themselves in the growing market for well-being and personal development. This business idea appeals to a broad target group, ranging from young adults to older people, and is meeting with increasing interest in methods to reduce stress and promote physical health.

A key to success in this area is to develop a unique concept that stands out from other offerings. This could include specialising in certain styles of yoga or meditation practices, integrating wellness services or creating a community through regular events and workshops. Choosing a suitable location that is both easily accessible and welcoming will go a long way to making the studio attractive.

Digitalisation offers additional opportunities to expand and diversify the business model. Offering online courses or developing an app that provides meditation sessions and yoga exercises at home can increase the reach and provide an alternative source of income. This enables customers to access the services regardless of time and place and promotes customer loyalty.

The marketing strategy should include both traditional and digital channels in order to reach a broad target group. Utilising social media, running targeted online advertising campaigns and attending local events can be effective ways to raise awareness of the offer. Customer reviews and recommendations play a crucial role in attracting new customers and should be actively encouraged.

Another important aspect is creating a strong community around the studio or courses. Encouraging interaction between participants and creating a sense of belonging can help to build a loyal customer base. This can be achieved through regular events, special offers for regular customers or an active presence on social networks.

The quality of the courses offered and the expertise of the teachers are crucial for long-term success. Investments in training and ongoing staff development ensure a high level of service and promote customer confidence. Clear communication of the studio's philosophy and values also helps it to stand out from the competition.

To summarise, setting up a yoga studio or offering meditation courses is a promising business idea for start-ups who want to combine a passion for well-being and personal development with entrepreneurial skills. By combining a unique concept with a strong marketing strategy and building a committed community, the foundations for a successful business can be laid.

Services to promote relaxation and mental well-being

The promotion of relaxation and mental well-being has become a key need in today's fast-paced society. This presents an excellent opportunity for start-ups to develop innovative services that target this growing need. By combining traditional techniques and modern technologies, entrepreneurs can create unique offerings that provide both physical and mental relief.

A key factor for success in this area is developing a deep understanding of the various stressors people face today and devising customised solutions to counteract them. This could include, for example, setting up a relaxation centre that offers a variety of techniques such as guided meditation, aromatherapy, sound therapy and mindfulness training. By creating a calm and welcoming space, customers can find a retreat from the stresses of everyday life.

In addition, the use of digital platforms opens up new opportunities to provide relaxation and wellbeing services. The development of apps or online platforms that offer personalised meditation and relaxation programmes allows users to access these resources anytime, anywhere. These digital offerings can be complemented by interactive elements, such as progress trackers or personalised recommendations, to improve the user experience and promote customer loyalty.

The effective marketing of these services plays a crucial role in their success. By utilising social media and content marketing, start-ups can build a strong online presence that increases the visibility of the offering and appeals to potential customers. Success stories and testimonials from satisfied customers can help build trust in the services offered.

Another way to differentiate yourself in this sector is to tailor your programmes to specific target groups, such as working people, students or parents. By taking into account the particular challenges and needs of these groups, tailor-made programmes can be developed that offer real added value.

The quality and effectiveness of the services offered are crucial for customer satisfaction and long-term loyalty. Continuous evaluation and customisation of services based on customer feedback and the latest research in mental health and relaxation techniques ensures that services remain relevant and effective.

To summarise, services to promote relaxation and mental wellbeing offer a promising business idea for start-ups based on the growing awareness of the importance of mental health and wellbeing. By combining innovative approaches, effective marketing and a strong focus on the needs of the target group, successful businesses can be established in this growing market segment.

Massage therapy

Offering massage services to reduce stress and promote physical health is an attractive model for start-ups. This business model appeals to a broad target group that is increasingly aware of the importance of well-being and the need to reduce stress. However, the successful implementation of this model requires careful planning and strategy.

Firstly, training and certification in various massage techniques is crucial. A deep understanding of the anatomy of the human body and the ability to recognise and respond to individual needs form the basis for high-quality massage services. Specialisations, such as sports massage, Swedish massage or reflexology, can differentiate the offer and make it more attractive to customers.

The choice of location plays a key role in success. A quiet, easily accessible location that offers a relaxing atmosphere is ideal. For start-ups on a limited budget, a mobile massage practice offering services at clients' homes or workplaces can be a cost-effective alternative. This flexibility can be especially attractive to working professionals who have difficulty scheduling time for such services.

Marketing massage services is critical to building a broad customer base. A strong online presence through a professional website, active social media channels and engagement in local communities can increase visibility. Referral programmes and partnerships with local businesses, gyms and health centres can also help attract customers.

A key element of the business model is the creation of a comprehensive customer experience. This includes not only the quality of the massage itself, but also the customer service before and after the treatment. Personalised advice, consideration of personal preferences and the offer of additional wellness services, such as aromatherapy or hot stones, can increase the value of the service.

The introduction of flexible pricing and package options can increase the attractiveness of the service. Offers for first-time customers, subscription models or packages for multiple sessions can attract customers and contribute to customer loyalty.

For long-term success, it is important to focus on the continuous improvement and expansion of services. This can include regular participation in further training, expanding the range of services to include additional wellness services or collaborating with professionals from related fields, such as physiotherapists or nutritionists.

To summarise, offering massages to reduce stress and promote physical health offers a promising business model for start-ups. By combining high-quality services, effective marketing and an excellent customer experience, entrepreneurs can operate successfully in this growing market segment.

Mental health, psychological counselling and therapy

In most countries, practising as a psychologist or psychotherapist is subject to certain requirements. These usually include a relevant university degree and a state licence or recognition. Online therapy providers must ensure that all therapists involved have the necessary qualifications and licences. This option of setting up a business will therefore not be discussed further here.

Coaching services

In the context of developing health apps and online platforms aimed at managing stress, anxiety and other psychological issues, technology and innovation play a key role. Healthcare start-ups that focus on these areas can have a significant impact on improving the mental health and wellbeing of society.

Development of health apps

The development of digital health solutions, especially apps for fitness tracking, health monitoring and mental wellbeing, is an attractive business model for start-ups that harbours significant growth potential. In a world where the demand for digital health solutions is constantly increasing, there are immense opportunities for innovations that can directly influence the well-being of users. For such ventures to succeed, it is crucial to develop a deep understanding of key areas such as user-friendliness, data protection, the scientific basis of content and the integration of gamification elements and personalisation.

User-friendliness takes centre stage in order to ensure long-term use and positive reviews. An app that can be used intuitively and without extensive familiarisation is more likely to become an integral part of users' everyday lives. At the same time, data protection is of the utmost importance, especially in the sensitive area of health data. Users must be able to rely on their personal information being secure and treated confidentially. This trust is fundamental to the acceptance and distribution of the app.

A scientific basis for the content and recommendations offered is just as critical. Users are looking for solutions that not only promise to improve their health and wellbeing, but do so on a sound, evidence-based foundation. Collaboration with subject matter experts and continuous updating of content is therefore essential to ensure the relevance and accuracy of the app.

The integration of gamification elements can be a key to success by increasing users' motivation to use the app regularly. Personalised content and recommendations based on users' individual data and preferences also contribute to the app's effectiveness and appeal. By using technologies such as artificial intelligence and machine learning, these personalisations can be implemented in innovative ways, further improving the user experience.

For start-ups that want to establish themselves in this field, it is essential to develop a clear vision for their app and combine this with a well thought-out market strategy. Understanding the target group, a strong positioning in the market and effective marketing measures are just as important as the willingness to respond to user feedback and continuously improve the app. Only in this way can a health app not only achieve commercial success, but also make a valuable contribution to improving the health situation and well-being of users.

Online platforms

The creation of online health and wellness communities and offerings is instrumental in providing a platform for peer-to-peer sharing, support and growth. These digital spaces allow individuals, regardless of their geographic location, to access information, resources and communities that focus on their specific mental and physical health needs and interests.

Services such as online counselling, virtual workshops and courses focused on stress management, mindfulness training and self-help strategies play an essential role in modern healthcare. These services not only offer users the opportunity to improve their knowledge and skills to overcome health challenges, but also promote a sense of belonging and being understood within the community.

The integration of online counselling services allows users to access professional support without the barriers that can come with traditional forms of counselling, such as appointments, travel and the stigma that can be associated with seeking help. These low-threshold services can provide initial counselling and, if necessary, lead to further professional help.

Virtual workshops and courses offer structured learning opportunities that help participants to learn and apply specific techniques and strategies. Topics range from stress management and mindfulness to nutritional counselling and physical fitness. The flexibility and accessibility of these programmes allow users to integrate them into their daily lives and promote personal growth.

A key element for the success of such platforms is the creation of a supportive and inclusive community. By building forums, group discussions and interactive features, users can share experiences, give and receive advice and find emotional support. These communities can foster a sense of belonging and help reduce the feeling of isolation that often accompanies health challenges.

For health and wellness start-ups, the key to success lies in developing platforms that not only provide high-quality, evidence-based content, but also foster a strong community culture. Consideration of user experience, privacy and security are paramount. In addition, continuous adaptation and expansion of offerings based on community feedback and needs are crucial to ensure relevant and effective support.

To summarise, online communities and offers in the field of health and wellness provide a unique opportunity to bring together people who are looking for or want to offer support. For start-ups, these platforms not only offer the potential for a sustainable business model, but also the chance to have a positive impact on the well-being and quality of life of many people.

For start-ups without capital, it is particularly important to pursue lean start-up strategies, seek partnerships and consider crowdfunding or other financing models if necessary. Involving potential users in product development at an early stage can help to validate the offering and utilise resources efficiently.

Education and training

Language and cultural coaching

Language and cultural coaching is an innovative business model that offers great potential for start-ups, especially in our globalised world where people are increasingly moving abroad for professional or personal reasons. This business model aims to support people moving to a new country or learning a new language, not only linguistically but also culturally. This comprehensive support helps people to settle into their new environment more effectively, avoid cultural misunderstandings and build a deeper connection with their new home.

A key aspect of language and cultural coaching is individualised support. Unlike traditional language courses or integration programmes, which often take a general approach, coaching allows for personalised and tailored support. Coaches can cater to the specific needs and challenges of each individual, whether in a professional context, in everyday life or in social interactions.

Services under this business model can be diverse and range from customised language training covering specific dialects or jargon to advice on local customs, etiquette and cultural norms. In addition, workshops and seminars can be offered that delve deeper into cultural topics such as the history, art, cuisine and holidays of the destination country.

Another important aspect is the use of modern technologies and platforms to maximise the reach and effectiveness of coaching. Online coaching sessions, virtual cultural workshops and language-specific learning apps can enrich the learning experience and enable clients to access services regardless of their location. In addition, social media and online communities can be utilised to create a platform for peer-to-peer exchange and networking, further promoting integration into the new culture.

Market knowledge and cultural competence are crucial for entrepreneurs who want to start a business in the field of language and cultural coaching. They must not only have extensive knowledge of the language(s) and culture(s) they wish to teach, but also effective coaching methods and pedagogical skills. In addition, it is important to have a solid understanding of the needs and expectations of the target audience in order to provide relevant and engaging services.

Successfully running a language and cultural coaching business also requires a strong online presence and marketing strategy to make potential clients aware of the services on offer. Content marketing, such as blog posts, videos and podcasts about cultural differences and language learning strategies, can help to generate interest and demonstrate the company's expertise.

To summarise, the language and cultural coaching business model offers an exciting opportunity for start-ups who have a passion for languages and cultures and want to help others find their way in a new environment. By providing customised services and using digital technologies, they can not only build a successful business but also have a positive impact on the lives of people who are in a period of transition and adjustment.

Courses and workshops

Using your own expertise to create and offer online or face-to-face courses in areas such as languages, music, art or fitness is an excellent business idea for start-ups. Platforms such as Udemy or Teachable have made it much easier to enter this market by providing a user-friendly infrastructure that allows experts to share their knowledge with a global audience. This approach offers numerous advantages and opens up a wide range of opportunities for budding entrepreneurs.

One of the biggest advantages of this business strategy is its flexibility and scalability. Once created, course content can be sold again and again without incurring additional costs or significant overheads for each new participant. This allows course providers to generate passive income while they can focus on creating new content or improving existing courses.

Another advantage is the wide range of potential topics and target groups. Whether it's language lessons, music lessons, art workshops or fitness classes, there are people around the world who are interested in learning new skills or improving existing ones. This presents a huge market opportunity for experts in almost any specialism.

The use of platforms such as Udemy and Teachable also offers the advantage that no extensive technical knowledge is required to create and manage online courses. These platforms offer simple tools for course design, payment processing and communication with course participants. In addition, course providers benefit from the existing user base of these platforms, which can reduce initial marketing and customer acquisition costs.

To be successful, however, start-ups should consider a few important aspects. Firstly, it is crucial to create high-quality and engaging course content that stands out from the competition. This can be achieved by integrating interactive elements, practical exercises and professionally produced teaching materials. In addition, an effective marketing strategy is important to increase the visibility of courses and attract potential participants. Social media platforms, content marketing and email marketing are just some of the tools that course providers can use to reach and engage their target audience.

Furthermore, start-ups should not underestimate the importance of feedback and continuous improvement. Obtaining feedback from course participants and adapting the courses based on this information can help to improve the quality of the programmes and increase customer satisfaction.

Overall, offering online or face-to-face courses in subject areas such as languages, music, art or fitness offers an exciting opportunity for start-ups to turn their passion and expertise into a profitable business. By utilising platforms such as Udemy or

Teachable, they can benefit from an established infrastructure and make their courses accessible to a global audience. With the right strategy, high-quality content and effective marketing, course providers have the opportunity to succeed in this growing market.

Retail and e-commerce

Affiliate marketing

Starting a blog or website with the aim of promoting products or services and earning commissions is an attractive way for start-ups to build an income. This endeavour, often known as affiliate marketing, relies heavily on choosing a specific niche that holds not only commercial potential, but also personal interest and passion. The challenge, and the key to success, lies in finding a balance between these aspects in order to develop a sustainable and engaging online presence.

The importance of choosing a niche cannot be overestimated. Choosing a niche that is close to your heart provides the natural motivation and perseverance needed to persevere through difficult times. At the same time, this niche must appeal to a large enough audience to ensure that the content produced will attract interest. Last but not least, the chosen field must offer sufficient commercial opportunities to ensure that the efforts pay off financially.

Building an engaged audience requires a strategic approach and patience. Quality content that offers real value is at the heart of any successful blog or website. By creating content that informs, entertains or inspires, you can gain a loyal readership. It is important to optimise content for search engines to promote visibility and organic growth.

The use of social media also plays a crucial role in developing an online presence. By regularly interacting and sharing content on the platforms favoured by the target audience, a direct connection with readers can be established. This not only encourages engagement, but also direct traffic to the website or blog.

In terms of monetisation, there are various ways to generate income in addition to affiliate marketing, such as through direct advertising, sponsored posts or the sale of your own products and services. A diversified income strategy helps to spread the financial risk and maximise sources of income.

The endeavour of making a blog or website successful is undoubtedly fraught with challenges, but also offers enormous potential for those willing to invest time, effort and passion. Success in this field requires consistency, the ability to adapt to changing trends and technologies, and a deep understanding of the needs and interests of the target audience. With the right approach and a clear focus, affiliate marketing can become a rewarding and sustainable source of income.

Online marketplace for local products

The idea of creating an online marketplace that connects local producers and artisans with customers interested in unique, handmade or locally produced products represents a contemporary response to the growing demand for authenticity, sustainability and local economic development. This business model taps into the trend of conscious consumption and provides a platform that not only supports sales, but also builds a community around the appreciation of local craftsmanship and production.

The first step for start-ups who want to take this route is careful planning and market research. It is important to understand which specific products or services are particularly in demand in the respective region or the chosen market segment. At the same time, a target group analysis should be carried out to determine the needs and preferences of potential customers. This not only helps with the positioning of the marketplace, but also with the design of the offer and the marketing strategy.

The technical realisation of such an online marketplace requires a user-friendly, reliable and scalable platform. The website or app should have an appealing design that reflects the values and aesthetics of the products on offer. Intuitive navigation, secure payment options and an efficient search function are crucial for a positive user experience. In addition, it is important to integrate mechanisms for reviews and feedback to promote trust and transparency on the platform.

A central aspect of setting up such a marketplace is the creation of a community of producers and craftspeople. This can be done by targeting and collaborating with local associations, cooperatives and networks. The platform should not only serve as a sales channel for these providers, but also offer support in the form of marketing, packaging and shipping. This creates a win-win situation in which local producers and artisans can increase their reach and visibility, while the marketplace offers unique and high-quality products.

Marketing and customer loyalty play a crucial role in the success of the marketplace. Strategies such as content marketing, social media and email marketing can be used to tell stories about the products, their makers and the manufacturing process. Such stories create an emotional connection with customers and emphasise the value of local, handmade products. Offers such as workshops, live demonstrations or visits to producers can also arouse interest and strengthen loyalty to the platform.

Ultimately, the realisation of such a project requires a combination of entrepreneurial vision, technical know-how and a deep understanding of local markets. Success depends on the ability to bridge the gap between traditional craftsmanship and modern consumer trends while pursuing sustainable and ethical business practices. With the right strategy and a dedicated team, an online marketplace for local producers and artisans can become an enriching resource for the community and a successful venture for start-ups.

Online sale of vintage and second-hand items

Collecting and selling vintage and second-hand items online offers start-ups an attractive business opportunity that taps into the growing interest in sustainability, uniqueness and history behind the products. Platforms such as eBay, Etsy or specialised social media channels have made it easier to reach a wide audience and market products effectively. This business idea combines a passion for finding unique finds with the potential to build a profitable online business.

Success in this business depends on several factors, starting with the ability to identify valuable and desirable items. Knowledge of different eras, styles and the quality of vintage and second-hand items is essential in order to select products that are in high demand. This also includes an understanding of which items are particularly popular with collectors and enthusiasts of special pieces.

The presentation of the items is also a crucial aspect. Good photography and detailed product descriptions that emphasise the history and condition of the item can increase the perceived value and make buyers more likely to purchase. It is important to be transparent about any defects to build trust with customers and encourage positive reviews.

Choosing the right sales platform is also important. While eBay offers a wide range of items and a large buyer base, Etsy is known for handmade, vintage and unique finds, attracting a specific target audience. Social media channels, especially Instagram and Facebook, have also established themselves as effective platforms for selling vintage and second-hand items, as they allow direct communication with interested parties and a visual presentation of the products.

Networking and relationships play a big role in this business. Networking with other sellers, participating in vintage markets and getting involved in community groups can help you find rare pieces and build a loyal buyer base.

In addition to physically searching for items, start-ups can enter into partnerships with local shops, flea markets and household clearances in order to be regularly supplied with new finds. This requires good negotiation skills and the ability to quickly assess the value of potential purchases.

Selling vintage and second-hand items online also requires careful planning in terms of logistics and customer care. This includes packaging and shipping items safely, handling returns and communicating with buyers to ensure a positive buying experience.

To summarise, selling vintage and second-hand items online offers an exciting business opportunity that not only provides financial benefits but also contributes to sustainability by counteracting the throwaway culture. With passion, knowledge and a strategic approach, start-ups can succeed in this area and build a loyal customer base that shares an appreciation for history and uniqueness.

E-learning platforms and content

The development of online courses or platforms that offer educational content in different formats opens up an exciting opportunity for start-ups to respond to the increasing demand for flexible, accessible and diverse learning opportunities. This approach makes it possible to cover a wide range of topics, from technical skills such as programming, web design and data analysis to soft skills such as communication, leadership and time management. By combining expertise and innovative technology, entrepreneurs can create educational products that have the potential to reach and support learners worldwide.

A key element in developing such courses or platforms is choosing the right format to deliver the learning content effectively. Video lessons, interactive exercises, live webinars, podcasts and PDF guides are just some of the many options available. The decision should be made based on the topic of the course, the learning objectives and the preferences of the target group. Videos, for example, are great for explaining complex concepts visually, while interactive exercises are particularly useful for developing practical skills.

The successful realisation of this business idea also requires thorough market research to understand the needs and preferences of the target group. This includes analysing the current trends in online education, assessing the competition and understanding which topics and skills are most in demand. Such research not only helps in designing the courses, but also in developing an effective marketing strategy to target the right learners.

Another important aspect is the creation of a user-friendly platform that facilitates access to the courses. Intuitive navigation, clear course structures and supportive learning resources are crucial to ensure a positive learning experience. In addition, it is important to build in mechanisms for feedback and interaction to foster a community of learners and enable ongoing engagement.

The quality and currency of educational content is also critical to success. Courses should be regularly reviewed and updated to ensure relevance and accuracy. The involvement of experts and professionals as course leaders or advisors can help to ensure the quality of content and build learner confidence.

Finally, it is important for start-ups to develop a solid monetisation strategy. There are various models, including individual course sales, subscriptions, company licences or the provision of free courses with the option of certificates for a fee. Choosing the right model depends on the goals of the platform, the preferences of the target group and the content offered.

To summarise, the development of online courses or educational platforms offers an excellent opportunity to gain a foothold in the growing field of online education. By combining high-quality content, a user-friendly platform and a well thought-out marketing strategy, start-ups can not only build a successful business, but also make a valuable contribution to the education and development of people worldwide.

Craft

Handmade products

For skilled craftspeople, making and selling handmade products offers a fascinating opportunity to turn their creativity and passion into a thriving business. Handmade products such as jewellery, artwork, handmade soaps or candles are particularly popular with consumers as they are looking for authenticity, quality and uniqueness that mass-produced products often cannot offer. Marketing these products via online platforms such as Etsy or at local markets opens up access to a broad and diverse customer base that shares an appreciation for craftsmanship.

The appeal of handmade products lies in their uniqueness and the story they tell. Customers are increasingly interested in buying products that have a personal touch and that they know have been made with care and attention to detail. This trend provides an excellent opportunity for artisans to sell their creations at a higher price, as customers are willing to pay for the quality and originality of these products.

The choice of selling platform is crucial for success. Etsy is one of the best-known platforms for handmade products and offers an established community of buyers who are specifically looking for handmade and unique items. The platform allows sellers to set up their own online shop, tell their stories and communicate directly with their customers. Etsy also offers various tools and resources to help sellers optimise their shops and market their products.

In addition to online platforms, selling at local markets is a great way to introduce products to a local audience and build personal relationships with customers. Local markets provide a platform to showcase products in a physical environment, giving customers the opportunity to directly experience and appreciate the quality of the handmade goods. This can also help to build a local following and generate word of mouth, which can be crucial to the long-term success of the business.

For success in this business, it is important to focus on the quality of the products, the uniqueness of the design and effective branding. Craftspeople should endeavour to develop a clear and appealing brand that reflects their philosophy and creative approach. A strong online presence, whether through a dedicated website, social media or both, is essential to increase visibility and engage with customers both locally and globally.

Finally, tradespeople should not underestimate the importance of customer engagement and excellent customer service. Positive customer reviews and recommendations can have a significant impact on success, so it's important to ensure high customer satisfaction and actively seek feedback.

To summarise, making and selling handmade products offers an exciting opportunity for crafty people to turn their passion into a profitable business. By using online platforms and local markets, focusing on quality and uniqueness, and building a strong brand and customer relationship, artisans can build a successful business that honours their creativity and craftsmanship.

Upcycling and restoration of furniture

The restoration and upcycling of old furniture into unique furnishings opens up a fascinating business opportunity for creative minds with skilled craftsmanship. This activity taps into the growing desire for sustainable, individualised living solutions and offers the opportunity to create something new and valuable from what is already there. At a time when there is a growing desire for authenticity and sustainability in design, the ability to transform forgotten pieces of furniture into desirable objects can represent a lucrative niche.

Success in this field depends heavily on the ability to recognise the beauty and potential in old or damaged pieces of furniture and to reinterpret them with creative skill and precision craftsmanship. Each piece of furniture thus becomes a work of art that not only tells a story, but also takes on a new function and a new life. This transformation appeals to a wide audience, from design lovers to environmentally conscious consumers who value the history and sustainability of objects in their living space.

Restored or upcycled items can be sold in a variety of ways. Online platforms offer a wide reach and the opportunity to target a specialised group of buyers. At the same time, social media provides a platform to share the creative process and build a community of like-minded people who share the values of handmade and reuse. Local markets and co-operations with furniture shops can also help to present the furniture to a local audience and receive direct feedback from customers.

An essential aspect of the business is the narrative that accompanies each piece. The story of the furniture's origin and transformation can significantly increase its value and deepen the emotional connection between the product and the buyer. These stories emphasise the uniqueness of each piece and highlight the craftsmanship and creative vision that has gone into the restoration and upcycling.

Interaction with customers and the ability to customise furniture according to individual wishes and needs offers another dimension of customer loyalty. This personalised approach not only extends the reach of your own range, but also promotes long-term relationships with a clientele that is looking for something special.

Restoring and upcycling furniture is therefore more than just a business; it is an art form that combines sustainability, craftsmanship and customised design. For those willing to apply their passion and craftsmanship, it offers the chance to embark on a meaningful and profitable journey that redefines the way we think about furniture and interior design.

Mobile car wash and valeting

Offering a mobile car wash and valeting service that comes directly to the customer is an attractive business idea that addresses the need for convenience and personalised service in today's fast-paced society. Customers increasingly value services that save them time while providing a high-quality service. A mobile car wash service fulfils exactly these criteria by bringing car care directly to the customer's doorstep, providing a flexible and time-saving solution for vehicle care.

Starting this business first requires careful planning and the procurement of the necessary cleaning equipment and materials. Basic equipment includes pressure washers, hoovers, microfibre cloths, buckets, brushes and a selection of cleaning and maintenance products specifically designed for car washing and valeting. Although the initial investment for this equipment is manageable, it is important to pay attention to quality to ensure effective and gentle cleaning.

One of the challenges of setting up a mobile car wash service is the logistics. Routes and appointments need to be planned efficiently to minimise time on the road and serve as many customers as possible. A well thought out schedule and the use of GPS navigation can help optimise travel times between customer locations.

Marketing and customer engagement are critical to the success of this business. A strong online presence, including a professional website and active social media channels, can help to raise awareness of the service and engage with potential customers. Customer reviews and recommendations also play an important role, as they strengthen the trust of new customers and emphasise the credibility of the service.

A special feature of the mobile car wash service is the ability to offer customised packages tailored to the specific needs and wishes of the customer. Whether a quick exterior wash or a comprehensive interior and exterior cleaning with additional care services - the flexibility to provide different service options can be an important competitive advantage.

In addition to the practical implementation of the service, it is important to focus on environmentally friendly practices. The use of biodegradable cleaning agents and water-saving washing methods appeals to customers who value sustainability and can set the company apart from other providers.

In summary, a mobile car wash and valeting service offers an excellent opportunity to enter the growing market for convenient and personalised services. With careful planning, high quality equipment and a strong focus on customer service and sustainability, this business model can be successful and build a loyal customer base.

Bicycle repair and maintenance

A mobile bike repair and maintenance service is an excellent business idea for start-ups with basic mechanical skills and a set of tools who want to get started with relatively low upfront costs. At a time when sustainability and health awareness are taking centre stage, the use of bicycles is steadily increasing. This creates a growing demand for convenient and accessible repair and maintenance services that come directly to the customer.

The key to the success of a mobile bike repair service lies in its ability to provide high quality services that are both efficient and convenient. Mobility allows customers to be reached where it is most convenient for them, be it at home, at work or even on their cycle route. This approach saves customers time and effort, making the service particularly attractive.

To start a mobile bike repair service, in addition to basic mechanical skills, you need a reliable set of tools and possibly spare parts. Investing in high-quality tools pays off in the long run, as they make the work easier and minimise the risk of damage to the customer's bike. In addition, it is important to undergo continuous training and keep up to date in order to be able to offer a wide range of repairs.

Marketing and customer acquisition are crucial to building the business. A professional website that clearly displays the services and prices offered, as well as an active social media presence, can help reach potential customers and raise awareness of the service. Word of mouth is also a powerful tool; satisfied customers are likely to recommend the service to others, opening up new business opportunities.

A special feature of the mobile bike repair service is the ability to offer customised maintenance packages tailored to the customer's needs and budget. This can range from simple repairs and adjustments to comprehensive maintenance work. Flexibility in the services and prices offered can help to appeal to a wider range of customers.

In addition, it is important to establish an efficient workflow and good scheduling in order to serve as many customers as possible without compromising the quality of the work. Careful planning and route optimisation can help to minimise journey times and maximise productivity.

A focus on environmentally friendly practices can also be a unique selling point that appeals to customers who value sustainability. Using environmentally friendly cleaning agents and lubricants or offering recycling options for old parts and tyres can reinforce the environmentally conscious image of the service.

Validation of the business idea - Volume 3

The validation of a business idea is the subsequent step for start-ups that lays the foundation for the future success of a company. All this and much more, such as financing issues, legal problems, etc. - are the subject of the 3rd and final volume in this series.

Here is a brief foretaste:

Firstly, it is essential to have a clear and precise definition of the business idea. A well-formulated business idea should summarise the problem to be solved, the target group and the proposed solution in one sentence. This not only makes it easier to communicate the idea to stakeholders and investors, but also serves as a starting point for validation.

Conducting market research helps to understand the actual demand and interest in the market. Techniques such as surveys, market analyses and the evaluation of trend data are essential. At the same time, competitors should be analysed and possible gaps in the market identified to ensure the uniqueness and competitiveness of the idea.

An in-depth target group analysis is also of great importance. By segmenting the target group, specific needs, preferences and behaviours can be understood. Obtaining direct customer feedback through interviews, focus groups or prototype tests provides valuable insights into the customer perspective.

A further step is the development of a minimal viable product (MVP). This simple but functional product model is used to test the assumptions about the business model with minimal resources and to quickly generate learning results that can be used to further develop the product.

Testing the business model using methods such as lean startup, A/B testing and evaluating different pricing strategies helps to assess profitability and market acceptance. At this stage, it is important to conduct a financial viability analysis that includes a break-even analysis and takes into account the estimated start-up and operating costs.

The data collected and the feedback from customers can provide an opportunity to adapt the business idea. The flexibility and willingness to iterate on the basis of these insights are crucial for further development. Start-ups must be prepared to modify their concept or even take a fundamentally new direction if the data suggests this.

Finally, the decision must be made as to whether the business idea should be pursued, adapted or discarded. This decision should be based on a balanced consideration of the knowledge gained, the financial prospects and also the personal commitment to the idea. The process of validating a business idea is therefore not only a challenge, but also an opportunity to set the right course for success in entrepreneurship.

But all of this is explained and discussed in detail in the third volume.